GET THINGS GOING

85 ASSET-BUILDING ACTIVITIES

FOR WORKSHOPS, PRESENTATIONS, AND MEETINGS

Susan Ragsdale and Ann Saylor

SEARCH INSTITUTE PRESS

Get Things Going
85 Asset-Building Activities for Workshops,
Presentations, and Meetings
Susan Ragsdale and Ann Saylor

At the time of publication, all facts and figures cited herein are the most current available; all telephone numbers, addresses, and website URLs are accurate and active; all publications, organizations, websites, and other resources exist as described in this book; and all efforts have been made to verify them. The authors and Search Institute make no warranty or guarantee concerning the information and materials given out by organizations or content found at websites that are cited herein, and we are not responsible for any changes that occur after this book's publication. If you find an error or believe that a resource listed herein is not as described, please contact Client Services at Search Institute.

Printed on acid-free paper in the United States of America.

Search Institute

Minneapolis, MN 55413
www.search-institute.org
612-376-8955 • 800-888-7828

ISBN-13: 978-1-57482-489-6

The activities "True Headings," "Sentence Puzzles," "Missed Signals," "Team Continuum Dialogue," "Intersections," "Electric Current," and "Youth Continuum Dialogue" were adapted with permission from protocols by the National School Reform Faculty Harmony Education Center (www.nsrfharmony.org). Activities contributed by other individuals are credited individually and used with permission.

Credits
Book Design: Jeenee Lee
Production Supervisor: Mary Ellen Buscher

Library of Congress
Cataloging-in-Publication Data
Ragsdale, Susan.
    Get things going : 85 asset-building activities for workshops, presentations, and meetings / Susan Ragsdale and Ann Saylor.
        p. cm.
Includes index.
ISBN-13: 978-1-57482-489-6 (pbk.)
ISBN-10: 1-57482-489-9 (pbk.)
1. Youth development. 2. Developmental psychology. I. Saylor, Ann. II. Title.
HQ796.R234 2011
305.235'5071--dc23
                                    2011033906

About Search Institute Press
Search Institute Press is a division of Search Institute, a nonprofit organization that offers leadership, knowledge, and resources to promote positive youth development. Our mission at Search Institute Press is to provide practical and hope-filled resources to help create a world in which all young people thrive. Our products are embedded in research, and the 40 Developmental Assets— qualities, experiences, and relationships youth need to succeed—are a central focus of our resources. Our logo, the SIP flower, is a symbol of the thriving and healthy growth young people experience when they have an abundance of assets in their lives.

CONTENTS

DEDICATION AND ACKNOWLEDGMENTS

This resource is dedicated to and built on the contributions of those who made the first edition of this book possible. To Karen Atkinson, Tim Duffey, Emily Foster, Rebecca Grothe, Merry Klemme, Nancy Leyerzapf, Shirley Luce, Marilyn Peplau, Derek Peterson, Clay Roberts, Cynthia Sowsnowski, Jim Williams, and Bob Wittman, thank you for the pioneering work you did.

To Jim Conway, Ruth Cox, Marilyn Peplau, Rick Jackson, Kelli Walker-Jones, Richard Hester, Bill Van de Griek, Laura Hansen, Louisa Avery, Janice Virtue, Cindy Lawrence, Laura Meverden, Travis Wright, Tara Brown, Anderson Williams, Julie Stevens, Mary Ackerman, and Flora Sanchez, thank you for your contributions and suggestions, which have greatly enriched this updated edition.

And to our partners at Search Institute Press who gave once again of their talents and expertise to make this the best resource possible: Tenessa, Karl, Phil, and Mary Ellen, thank you! You guys rock . . . every time! Last but not least, to our spouses (Ann's husband, Dan, and Susan's husband, Pete), thank you for believing in us, helping us manage life, giving us perspective, and being lifelong friends.

INTRODUCTION

Meetings and trainings; trainings and meetings! Our society runs on them as a way to communicate, educate, network, envision possibilities, and get things done. Often within these gatherings, someone is responsible for trying to get people on board with an idea or vision, get them to buy in, and encourage them to work together toward a desired end.

Do you need to kick off a meeting? Have you been asked to lead an activity to help a group get to know each other better? Are you doing a training that requires building community among strangers? Working on trust in your youth group? Looking for just the thing to help your staff team think about your impact at work?

If you said yes to any of these questions, then this book is for you. Be it meeting or training, *Get Things Going* has ideas to help your group get down to business with activities that are intended to help build community, respect and understanding, trust, and impact—four essential dimensions of thriving groups.

Within this book are tools and activities to get things going in a way that's not mundane. It provides processes that make an impact on group culture by changing the way it works and where it focuses attention.

This book recognizes that the challenge for any facilitator is to keep participants encouraged, motivated, and centered, while also helping equip them to have a deeper impact in their work. Facilitators often must balance getting across key information in a productive way with being interesting and engaging. At the same time, they must build the group as a unit.

The activities within these pages do just that. They get people moving and thinking and ideas flowing. And the book seeks to equip *you*, the called-upon facilitator, with activities that can help your group stay focused and "move" forward together as a team as they laugh, learn, and grow together. The activities are useful for any team setting, and particularly for individuals in the business of youth development and education.

THE BENEFITS OF PLAYING AS A PART OF THE WORK CULTURE

Games and experiential learning have their place in the business side of life, be that the staff meeting, boardroom, club gathering, or local PTO. They have a serious side that can advance the work of any group in a playful and purposeful way while simultaneously adding perspective and fresh energy. They keep work on the inspiring and interesting side. Games can change work culture in many beneficial ways. For instance, games

- level the playing field and create neutral spaces;
- build relationships;
- invite participants to interact in a way different from their daily routines;
- ease anxieties and increase comfort levels;
- involve and engage the whole person (mind, spirit, creativity, body);
- provide opportunities for everyone to speak up and out; and
- create teachable moments and offer safe venues for recognizing and addressing touchy situations or behaviors.

HOW TO USE THIS BOOK

Before you select an activity, ask yourself *why* you are playing. Are you setting the tone, creating a common experience, or homing in on a vision? Knowing your goal for what you want to accomplish will help you easily identify which activity fits best with your ultimate purpose.

The featured activities all target four areas of group culture that many teams (corporate, coalitions, staff teams, youth groups, parent groups) struggle with as they seek to stay purposeful, vision oriented, and authentic. These critical aspects of group development are *common experience, respect and understanding, trust,* and *impact.* The book is divided into sections based on these four areas for the purpose of helping you quickly identify the target area you want to address within your group.

Common Experience: This collection of icebreakers and games will develop and build on a sense of common ground so that all participants see themselves as part of a community (be it for a one-time training or an ongoing group) where they are welcome and know they belong and where they recognize that they have a lot to give to and receive from the shared experience that is vital for the whole community.

Embedded within this section is an important subsection called Asset Exploration. Foundational to a common experience, this section features activities that focus specifically on increasing participants' knowledge and understanding of the Developmental Assets® and their importance to positive youth development. Learn more about the assets on page 12.

Respect and Understanding: Cultivate this aspect through a variety of team-building activities that provide participants with an opportunity to gain a sense of the individual strengths that each person has and brings to a group, and to develop a healthy mutual appreciation for who each person is and what he or she is about.

Trust: Participants can learn and grow together in these activities that target the importance of developing and maintaining a lasting trust in working and being together.

Impact: This section offers an opportunity for exploration of beliefs, perspectives, and values about the group's work and the roles and impact each person can have. It also offers activities to help groups think through setting a vision and choosing strategies to move toward their vision.

ORGANIZATION OF THE GAMES

The description of each activity includes its purpose, estimated time, supplies needed, any preparation, directions, a wrap-up that includes key messages or discussion questions to highlight key elements, and asset categories associated with the activity. "Key elements" denote general issues addressed by the game, for example, *communication*, *creative problem solving*, *vision*, *team building*, or *celebration*. "Asset categories" tell you which aspect of positive human development you are emphasizing within your group, *and* it indicates which aspect you can zero in on if you or someone on your team decides to use or adapt an activity to use with youth.

KEY CHARACTERISTICS OF GAMES IN THIS BOOK

The games share several common traits. They are

1. wide-ranging (varied to reflect different learning styles);
2. adaptable (easily manipulated by changing the questions to fit the goal and the group);

3. low prep, low cost (for the sake of the facilitator's time, sanity, and budget);

4. interactive (by design to actively engage as many as possible in what's happening); and

5. purposeful (for getting business under way, meeting an objective, or "moving" the group forward in its own development even while it is being playful).

ROLE OF THE DEVELOPMENTAL ASSETS®

The Developmental Assets®, while they are steeped in research on positive youth development, offer up a common understanding of general human development and what we *all* need. The eight broad categories of assets name aspects of life that are good for us all, and that we all need in order to have healthy, happy lives. The longer we can engage with the assets and put them into practice together, the more we will understand on an intuitive, experiential, and practical level what promotes positive, healthy growth for youth. With that knowledge and understanding, we will be able to increase our impact with youth and each other.

Created by Search Institute and known as the building blocks of positive youth development that help young people grow up healthy, caring, and responsible, the assets empower youth both to thrive and to stay out of trouble. The more assets youth have, the more likely they are to be leaders in their communities, succeed in school, resist danger, maintain good health, and overcome trouble. The more assets, the merrier!

The eight broad categories, which are denoted throughout the book, are:

Support
Young people need to be surrounded by people who love, care for, appreciate, and accept them.

Empowerment
Young people need to feel valued and valuable. This happens when youth feel safe and respected.

Boundaries and Expectations
Young people need clear rules, consistent consequences for breaking rules, and encouragement to do their best.

Constructive Use of Time
Young people need opportunities—outside of school—to learn and develop new skills and interests with other youth and adults.

Commitment to Learning
Young people need a sense of the lasting importance of learning and a belief in their own abilities.

Positive Values
Young people need to develop strong guiding values or principles to help them make healthy life choices.

Social Competencies
Young people need the skills to interact effectively with others, to make difficult decisions, and to cope with new decisions.

Positive Identity
Young people need to believe in their own self-worth and to feel that they have control over the things that happen to them.

For more information on the assets, go to www.search-institute.org.

What Are Developmental Assets?

Search Institute has identified 40 building blocks of development that help young people grow up healthy, caring, and responsible. The more of these Developmental Assets young people have, the more likely they are to be leaders in their communities, succeed in school, resist danger, maintain good health, and overcome trouble. Youth who say they have assets are also less likely to abuse drugs, skip school, fight, or attempt suicide.

EXTERNAL ASSETS

SUPPORT

1. **Family Support**—Family life provides high levels of love and support.

2. **Positive Family Communication**—Young person and her or his parent(s) communicate positively, and young person is willing to seek advice and counsel from parent(s).

3. **Other Adult Relationships**—Young person receives support from three or more non-parent adults.

4. **Caring Neighborhood**—Young person experiences caring neighbors.

5. **Caring School Climate**—School provides a caring, encouraging environment.

6. **Parent Involvement in Schooling**—Parent(s) are actively involved in helping the child succeed in school.

EMPOWERMENT

7. **Community Values Youth**—Young person perceives that adults in the community value youth.

8. **Youth as Resources**—Young people are given useful roles in the community.

9. **Service to Others**—Young person serves in the community one hour or more per week.

10. **Safety**—Young person feels safe at home, at school, and in the neighborhood.

BOUNDARIES AND EXPECTATIONS

11. **Family Boundaries**—Family has clear rules and consequences and monitors the young person's whereabouts.

12. **School Boundaries**—School provides clear rules and consequences.

13. **Neighborhood Boundaries**—Neighbors take responsibility for monitoring young people's behavior.

14. **Adult Role Models**—Parent(s) and other adults model positive, responsible behavior.

15. **Positive Peer Influence**—Young person's best friends model responsible behavior.

16. **High Expectations**—Both parent(s) and teachers encourage the young person to do well.

CONSTRUCTIVE USE OF TIME

17. **Creative Activities**—Young person spends three or more hours per week in lessons or practice in music, theater, or other arts.

18. **Youth Programs**—Young person spends three or more hours per week in sports, clubs, or organizations at school and/or in community organizations.

19. **Religious Community**—Young person spends one hour or more per week in activities in a religious institution.

20. **Time at Home**—Young person is out with friends "with nothing special to do" two or fewer nights per week.

INTERNAL ASSETS

COMMITMENT TO LEARNING

21. **Achievement Motivation**—Young person is motivated to do well in school.

22. **School Engagement**—Young person is actively engaged in learning.

23. **Homework**—Young person reports doing at least one hour of homework every school day.

24. **Bonding to School**—Young person cares about her or his school.

25. **Reading for Pleasure**—Young person reads for pleasure three or more hours per week.

POSITIVE VALUES

26. **Caring**—Young person places high value on helping other people.

27. **Equality and Social Justice**—Young person places high value on promoting equality and reducing hunger and poverty.

28. **Integrity**—Young person acts on convictions and stands up for her or his beliefs.

29. **Honesty**—Young person "tells the truth even when it is not easy."

30. **Responsibility**—Young person accepts and takes personal responsibility.

31. **Restraint**—Young person believes it is important not to be sexually active or to use alcohol or other drugs.

SOCIAL COMPETENCIES

32. **Planning and Decision Making**—Young person knows how to plan ahead and make choices.

33. **Interpersonal Competence**—Young person has empathy, sensitivity, and friendship skills.

34. **Cultural Competence**—Young person has knowledge of and comfort with people of different cultural/racial/ethnic backgrounds.

35. **Resistance Skills**—Young person can resist negative peer pressure and dangerous situations.

36. **Peaceful Conflict Resolution**—Young person seeks to resolve conflict nonviolently.

POSITIVE IDENTITY

37. **Personal Power**—Young person feels he or she has control over "things that happen to me."

38. **Self-Esteem**—Young person reports having a high self-esteem.

39. **Sense of Purpose**—Young person reports that "my life has a purpose."

40. **Positive View of Personal Future**—Young person is optimistic about her or his personal future.

COMMON EXPERIENCE

COLOR FOCUS

Purpose: To get participants thinking about the power of focus and perspective on their actions

Estimated Time: 10 minutes

Supplies: None

Directions: Inform participants that they will be doing important work during this session. Say, "I want to get your brains geared and ready. So, in order to prepare, we're going to do an exercise in memory."

Instruct everyone to get up and walk around the room for 90 seconds, and make a mental note of everything red (or whatever color) in the room. They can't write down the items on paper or make any kind of notes other than mental notes.

Make a big deal of the time—note the starting time, 60 seconds left, 30 seconds left, etc.

Ask participants to pair up. Tell them that you want them to close their eyes and, without opening their eyes, talk together, or let each person list individually what he or she saw. Ask them to share everything blue (or whatever color that is different from the given color) that they remember.

Wrap-up:
- How many of you had difficulty naming objects that were blue? Raise your hand.
- Why was that?
- How often do we see what we are looking for?

This activity is a simple illustration of how we tend to see what we look for. When it comes to our work with young people, we can choose what we look for and what we emphasize. We can choose to focus on the strengths and gifts we see in young people, or we can anticipate seeing the bad things. It's all a matter of perspective. How will you focus on seeing the good things this week?

Key Elements: Communication, Vision, Community Building

Asset Categories: Boundaries and Expectations, Social Competencies

Insider's Tip: You can make the same point with any subject matter: when you look for people wearing polka dots, you see people wearing polka dots; when you look for minivans, you see minivans; when you look for people in real need, you see people in real need.

Activity contributed by Jim Conway, Madison, Wisconsin

NAME TAG SANDWICH

Purpose: To get participants thinking about the power of their influence and how others have influenced them

Estimated Time: 10 minutes

Supplies: Plain name tags and writing utensils

Directions: Ask each participant to write her name in the middle of a name tag, leaving space above and below her name.

Invite everyone to recall people who have had a positive impact on their lives in small ways and big ways. Tell them to write the name of one such person in small letters under their names.

Next, ask participants to identify a youth or adult for whom they are role models. Ask them to write the name of that person in small letters above their names.

Invite participants to mingle around the room to talk about the people on their name tag and listen to the stories of others.

Wrap-up: Note that each one of us can be an important link in strengthening and supporting others. The people who had a positive impact on our lives when we were young can serve as examples for how we can show the people in our lives we care. We build on those who served as a foundation for our growth and development. They lifted us up. We hold up those we want to support as they grow and develop. In this way, we pass on from generation to generation what we hope to build within each young person. We pass on a legacy of strong youth and hope for future growth.

Key Elements: Communication, Team Building, Celebration, Community Building

Asset Categories: Support, Empowerment, Boundaries and Expectations, Social Competencies, Positive Identity

Activity contributed by Marilyn Peplau, New Richmond, Wisconsin

CONNECTIONS

Purpose: To start building common ground among diverse team members

Estimated Time: 6–8 minutes

Supplies: None

Directions: Instruct players to mingle with as many people as they can in 3–5 minutes, exchanging names and finding something they have in common beyond their professional lives. For example, they might find that they share common interests in favorite foods, activities they enjoy, pets, or number of siblings. Each person should try to remember both the names and the connections he made with each other person.

At the end of the time allotted, ask if they remember how many people they met. Determine who met the most people.

Ask who can remember the names of every person they met *and* the thing(s) they had in common with each person. Ask for a volunteer to name each person he met *and* the thing(s) he had in common with each person. Celebrate participants' efforts!

Wrap-up:
- How does building connections help build a supportive team atmosphere for our group?
- How does having connections change the way we work together?

Key Elements: Communication, Celebration, Team Building, Community Building

Asset Categories: Support, Social Competencies, Positive Identity

Adapted from Great Group Games for Kids *by Susan Ragsdale and Ann Saylor*

BEHIND EVERY NAME

Purpose: To help participants learn each other's names and more about their background

Estimated Time: 8–12 minutes

Supplies: None

Directions: Ask participants to form groups of three with people they don't know well or haven't talked with much today. Instruct these triads to share in their small groups their names and the story behind their names. Broaden their thoughts by saying something like this: "Were you named after someone or for a particular reason? Is there a cool story about your name? Is it a family name? Do you like or dislike your name? Would you prefer another name? If so, what would that name be?"

Tell them they have 3–4 minutes for each person in the triad to talk about his name.

When time is up, ask if anyone wants to introduce someone in her triad to the big group and tell a little bit about that person's name.

Wrap-up: If the group members know each other well, ask if anyone discovered something new about her colleagues or has common ground he didn't realize before.

Ask the group why they think we took the time to dig a little deeper into each other's names and backgrounds.

Note to the group that names are important. Being known is important. Names speak to who we are. Knowing how people want to be named shows respect for who they are and what they want. Being able to call people by their names—and pronounce them correctly—expresses care and value. Knowing names and using them is a simple strategy to help both youth and adults feel welcomed and feel like part of a community. Taking the time to find out more about people, even those we may see every day, helps us to know them and understand who they are.

Key Elements: Communication, Celebration, Community Building

Asset Categories: Social Competencies, Positive Identity

Insider's Tip: This is a good activity for challenging groups to go beyond names and learn more about one another. It is also good for intentionally engaging in learning, remembering, and sharing with others correct pronunciations of names and/or what people want to be called, which may not be widely known within a group.

Adapted from Great Group Games *by Susan Ragsdale and Ann Saylor*

THE POTLUCK NAME GAME

Purpose: To help participants learn one another's names

Estimated Time: 10–15 minutes

Supplies: None

Directions: Have the group make one big circle of 15 people. If the group is larger than that, divide the group into smaller circles of 6 to 15 people each. Tell them that you are planning a potluck/picnic; they are all invited, and you need to know what they are bringing. Each person will bring an item that starts with the same sound as his first name. For example, Sam might bring spinach, Mary might bring milk, and Fernando might bring figs.

Have someone in the circle introduce himself and say what he will bring. Sam, for example, would say, "I'm Sam, and I'll bring spinach." The group responds by repeating back to Sam, "Spinach Sam." Continue to the next person and let her introduce herself; the group repeats her menu item and name. Then start over from the beginning and say, "Spinach Sam" plus the new person's menu item and name. Continue all the way around the circle.

Wrap-up: Relationships are key to everything—feeling welcome, the sense of being part of a team or community, the foundation from which impact occurs. Good relationships start from taking time to know each other. Knowing each other's names is that first step toward possibility—the possibility of what can be as we know each other and work together.

Key Elements: Communication, Community Building, Fun, Working Together

Asset Categories: Support, Social Competencies

Insider's Tip: Association is one of the best tricks for learning names. It's useful for learning names in a group that will be together for a short time—in a workshop or a one-day team-building event, for example—and it helps lock in names for groups that will be together for the long haul. Regardless of how long the group has been together, it never hurts to do a name game to break the ice and also to help you learn who's in the room.

Adapted from "Who's Coming to Snacks and Play?" in Great Group Games for Kids *by Susan Ragsdale and Ann Saylor*

CURIOUS QUESTIONS

Purpose: To help participants engage in conversation about things they really want to know and to move the group beyond the obvious knowledge of what is going on in the group

Estimated Time: 8–15 minutes

Supplies: Scrap paper and a pencil for each person

Directions: Ask each person to quickly jot down three questions to ask people in the room during one-on-one conversations. Challenge participants to go beyond the usual fallback questions like "What is your name?" "What agency or program do you work with?" or "What is your position?" Rather, encourage them to get creative and be curious. What do they really want to know about others in the room? What is important to them and what do they value? What silly things have they always wondered about that will help them know and understand others better? They may have questions about hobbies or silly moments, or they may want to ask about beliefs, inspirations, or treasured life moments. Give participants 2 minutes to generate their questions.

When time is up, ask participants to stand, mingle, greet others, ask their questions, let their new friends answer the questions, then answer the questions asked of them. After 6–8 minutes of mingling, regroup and ask participants to share some of the things they learned about one another.

Wrap-up: In this activity, participants got to ask questions they really wanted to know about the other people in the room. Those questions probably were inspired by things that are important to them or that they were curious about, or by a sense of humor.

It's important for us to create space and dedicate time to really get to know the heart of who we are as people and as a team. The more we get to know each other, the more likely we are to find common ground and begin to truly understand each other—where each of us is coming from and what's important to us. With deeper connections and conversations come understanding, respect, and trust. With those elements come better teamwork and greater impact: *I know you. I know what you care about—what is important to you. I understand where you are coming from. And you know me.* When we know each other's cores, we can trust that that's how we'll show up to do our work. We understand what drives each of us—how we are alike and how we are different— and we can accept that.

Key Elements: Communication, Community Building, Teamwork

Asset Categories: Support, Social Competencies, Positive Identity

TABLETOP CONVERSATION STARTERS

Purpose: To help participants engage in dialogue and listen to each other

Estimated Time: 5–8 minutes

Supplies: Card stock and markers (alternate option: type questions or statements with a computer and print them out)

Preparation: Write a question or statement on each piece of card stock (or use a computer and printer) and fold the cards in half to make table tents. Place these table tents on tables before the meeting or training starts.

Conversation Starters:
What is something you've always wanted to know about your colleagues?
When I was in high school, one word that described me was . . .
The place you would find me after school was . . .
The activity that kept me grounded as a young person was . . .
The person who kept me grounded as a young person was . . .
If I wrote my autobiography, the title would be . . . because . . .
A movie title that describes my school/afterschool/teenage experiences is . . .
    because that experience was . . .
Legacy: what I most want to pass on to others is . . .
My best hope for youth is . . .
What I value most about our team (job, young people, community, agency) is . . .
What I need most from my teammates to be and do my best is . . .

Directions: Instruct participants to introduce themselves to the people at their table and discuss the conversation starter posted on their table for 5–7 minutes.

Note: If time is an issue, have participants turn to a neighbor for discussion, and shorten the amount of time allowed for conversation.

Option 2: As a pre-event activity, encourage participants to talk about the question or statement on their tabletop as they arrive.

Option 3: As you go around the room, have each participant say his name and talk about one of the conversation starters.

For **Options 1** and **2**, you can, throughout the meeting, randomly shuffle the table tents to start new conversations at each table. For instance, you can shuffle the table tents when participants are coming back from breaks or when you sense the agenda needs to shift in energy or focus.

Key Elements: Communication, Community Building

Asset Categories: Support, Social Competencies, Positive Identity

Insider's Tip: Table toppers are an easy way to start a group right into conversation. When participants enter a room, sit down, and see the table tents, they get curious and start thinking. Table toppers can pull their attention to the space you've created and get them ready to focus on what's going on in the room.

TRAIN OF CLUES

Purpose: To help participants name their own strengths and identify others' strengths

Estimated Time: 5–10 minutes

Supplies: Post-it Notes, pens

Directions: Have each person write on Post-it Notes four or five clues about who he is and how he contributes to the group (one clue per Post-it Note). For example, Bill may write on his five Post-it Notes that he

1. loves to create spaces where people can learn;
2. is very organized;
3. likes to make people feel welcome;
4. picks yummy snacks for meetings; and
5. asks clear, thought-provoking questions to apply learning for himself and for his work team.

Instruct participants not to let anyone else see what they are writing. When they are finished, each person gives one of her clues to you, the facilitator. You post these clues (no names attached!) in one area of the room. Participants mingle, looking for their own clues. When a person finds her clue, she secretly adds one of her remaining four clues to her first clue. Gradually adding the rest of her clues, one clue at a time, she creates a "train" of clues. As people read through the various clue trains, they can, at any time, stick a blank Post-it Note next to any given clue train and add the name of the person they think is the "engineer" (originator) of that clue train. The real engineer can come by later and covertly circle or star a correct guess or put an X through an incorrect guess.

Hint: Identifying the various identities can be done over time if your group meets regularly. Simply keep the clue trains posted, or transfer them onto a flip chart or poster board to bring out again at future meetings.

If your group is working together for a long period of time, consider keeping the lists of everyone's strengths as a reminder of each person's gifts and how you can best make use of her passions.

Wrap-up: In this activity, we can see the power of each individual: the gifts each one brings to a group. How powerful are we as a team when we work from our strengths? What are the possibilities of what we can do to make a difference in the lives of youth?

Key Elements: Communication, Team Building, Celebration, Community Building

Asset Categories: Social Competencies, Positive Identity, Empowerment

Insider's Tip: This activity pushes participants to think about how they contribute to the group and the gifts they offer that are part of who they are. It can lead into other activities that build on working together and solving problems creatively once each person's gifts are identified.

UNPACKING THE BAG

Purpose: To help participants identify their own strengths, energy, and energy zappers, as well as their personal vision and hopes

Estimated Time: 15–25 minutes

Supplies: Copies of "Unpacking the Bag Worksheet" (see page 25) and pens

Directions: Distribute the worksheet to participants and ask them to take 2 minutes to fill it out. When they are finished, ask participants to introduce themselves to the group by answering the questions.

Note: If time is a factor, have individuals introduce themselves to the others sitting at their tables, or have participants team up in pairs or triads.

For groups that know each other well, you can collect all the completed worksheets, read them aloud, and challenge your team to guess which person the answers describe.

Wrap-up: When we think about our work, it is important that we know who we are, the gifts we bring, our limits, and the vision toward which we work. Where are we in balance? Where do we need to get back on track? How well are we caring for ourselves? How well are we investing our time and energy in the things that matter the most to us? Where do we need to get clearer? To best serve others, it is important that we be authentic and serve from our gifts and our sense of calling. To have the best impact on youth, we must first know ourselves so that we can better guide them on how to discover their own gifts and sense of purpose.

Key Elements: Communication, Team Building, Community Building

Asset Categories: Commitment to Learning, Positive Identity, Empowerment, Positive Values

Insider's Tip: This activity helps participants identify core elements of their beings and values. It provides a snapshot they can use to examine their current view of themselves and life and to think about where they want to be and how who they are fits with their current priorities, choices, and activities.

Unpacking the Bag Worksheet

Instructions: Pack your suitcase/backpack with these core elements that go with you wherever you go in life.

- What do you love?

- What strength/skills/talents do you bring to any setting or group?

- What gives you energy?

- What keeps you sane?

- What is your destination?

- What did you purposefully choose *not* to pack?

- What do you want to take away from the trip?

- What are the things that get in the way of a good trip?

BIG WORLD, LITTLE WORLD

Purpose: To encourage participants to share the big and little things going on in their lives that hold their attention

Estimated Time: 5–10 minutes

Supplies: None, or a chair of honor (optional)

Directions: Start meetings with an "open mic" session, saying that you want to know what's going on in your team members' lives before everyone focuses on the task at hand. To "train" your group and get them used to this method, start out by asking the group in general, "What's going on in the big world?" Let people talk about what's going on in the news or in the community for 2–3 minutes (or as the spirit moves them). Follow up with the next question: "What's going on in your little world?" Ask people to share whatever they want about what's going on in their lives. Let them know that this will be an ongoing practice to start meetings so that team members can check in with each other on human and personal levels before turning to their tasks.

Hint: The leader of this activity can prompt conversations by following up on something that was said at a previous meeting or by observing new details. For example, you might say, "Hey, Rico! I heard you just started your basketball season. Anything else new going on in your life? Something you want to report?"

Variations:
- Ask all participants to share one thing that's going really well for them right now and one thing that they're working to improve.
- Ask participants to share the "highs" and "lows" (and maybe even the "really silly" moments) of the past week.

Sometimes the simplest of prompts may help someone who needs or wants to say something. Spending 5–10 minutes on caring for your team is a worthwhile investment that makes them feel supported and valued.

Key Elements: Communication, Team Building, Celebration, Creative Problem Solving

Asset Categories: Support, Empowerment, Social Competencies, Positive Values, Positive Identity

Insider's Tip: Incorporate this tried-and-true activity into ongoing meetings as a regular process to encourage a sense of unity, support, and caring for the members of your team. It also provides a transition from the outside world to what's going on in the meeting or training and allows participants speak their minds and hearts in order to clear some space for what is going to happen in the meeting.

Original idea contributed by Tara Brown, Nashville, Tennessee

30-SECOND SPOTLIGHT

Purpose: To provide a platform for participants to get to know each other on a more personal level as well as share what they believe is important

Estimated Time: 5 minutes or less

Supplies: Timer

Directions: Name a topic for table groups to talk about. Tell participants that each person will have 30 seconds of *uninterrupted* time to talk. The person who traveled the farthest to attend the meetings begins. Give a signal for the first speakers to start speaking, and after 30 seconds signal the next speakers to begin. Continue, keeping time until everyone has had a chance to speak.

Possible topics: Cooking, vacations, family, the weekend, hobbies, the best day ever, most prized possession, best book/movie ever

Wrap-up: Taking 30 seconds to talk or listen may not seem like much, but making the effort to connect with each other in small ways adds up to more powerful relationships. Listening and learning about each other leads to respect, understanding, and trust—key elements in working together successfully.

Option 2: 30-Second Stump Speech on Assets

Distribute the list of the 40 Developmental Assets (see page 12). Select one of the assets from the list and have someone read its definition aloud. Start the clock for the first speaker in each group to begin a 30-second presentation on how to build that asset or why that asset is important.

After 30 seconds, signal that time is up. Select another asset, read its definition, and start the time for the next person's stump speech. Repeat the process as many times as you wish.

Wrap-up: Taking 30 seconds to think about how we can make a difference in the lives of youth may not seem like much, but making an effort in multiple little ways every day adds up to a *real* difference in the lives of youth. It takes the many positive experiences and opportunities that we can share every day to help young people get what they need and deserve in order to be whole.

Key Elements: Communication, Celebration, Community Building, Team Building

Asset Categories: Support, Constructive Use of Time, Empowerment, Positive Identity, Commitment to Learning, Positive Values

Insider's Tip: This activity pushes people to speak on the spot, which can be challenging, but it is also informative and builds skill. Easy topics allow for comfort in practicing communication skills; inspirational topics allow participants to offer insights about particular assets and why they value them. Choose topics based on what you need to accomplish: build relationships, encourage lighthearted fun, or delve more deeply into the assets.

CORNER CHOICES

Purpose: To help participants reflect on their communication styles and preferences

Estimated Time: 5–8 minutes

Supplies: Copy of the categories list

Directions: Tell participants that you are going to read four choices and point to a corner of the room for each choice. They are to walk quickly to the area that represents their own personal choice. Once everyone has chosen, you read the next series of choices and participants choose again.

Once all the choices have been read (this is a fast-paced activity), point out the value of the activity (as described after the following list).

Categories
1. Vanilla Ice Cream, Chocolate Ice Cream, Butter Pecan Ice Cream, Frozen Yogurt
2. Dogs, Cats, Goldfish, Pet Rock
3. Beach, Mountains, Desert, Theme Park
4. Roller Coaster, Tilt-a-Whirl, Bumper Cars, Bench in the Shade
5. Football Game, Concert, Renaissance Fair, Theater
6. Coffee, White Chocolate Mocha, Peppermint Patty Latte, Green Tea
7. Buy It New, Buy It Used, Make It Myself, Do Without
8. Done Just Right, Done Well, Almost Done, Not Done
9. Conflict, Compromise, Avoidance, My Way!
10. Change, Status Quo, Leave It Alone, Whatever

Wrap-up:
- Which was the right answer in each of the categories?
- Was there a right answer?
- Did anyone worry when they were asked about vanilla versus chocolate?
- Did you worry when you were asked about conflict versus compromise?

This game is about you, who you are, what you like. It starts out with easy choices, then progresses to more serious, more personal things, but because we had been in the same process for all the items, you keep thinking in that same way. That thinking lets you say, "This is my style. This is where I'm coming from, and I'm confident to say that. This is what I like. This is who I am." Someone who chooses chocolate ice cream could say, "That's what I like. That's just me, who I am" and "I'm comfortable with that choice."

It's important to be comfortable with who you are. Remember that there is no right answer. Not being a leader or not wanting to be a leader is a statement of fact, just like preferring chocolate or vanilla. It is still a preference. Be okay with it; be part of the team as yourself. Show up each day as yourself, and know that *that* is good enough.

Key Elements: Communication, Celebration, Conflict Resolution, Creative Problem Solving

Asset Categories: Positive Identity, Social Competencies, Boundaries and Expectations

Insider's Tip: Since there is no discussion between movements, participants focus on what they know about themselves rather than on others. This keeps the game "safe" when more complicated choices are offered. And that's the goal—to get participants to be real about their choices without looking around the room for the right answer or where they think someone else (such as a boss or a best friend) wants them to go.

Activity contributed by Bill Van de Griek, Nashville, Tennessee

DIVERSITY BINGO

Purpose: To explore the strengths and diversity within a group

Estimated Time: 5–10 minutes

Supplies: Copies of bingo card, pens

Preparation: Make a bingo card by drawing five vertical columns and four horizontal rows. Place categories like these within each box of a bingo card, leaving room for people to sign each box: writing hand preference, hair color, sweet vs. salty, hometown (farm, city, rural), fine dining vs. fast food, bed made vs. unmade, talk vs. listen, country vs. rock 'n' roll, morning person vs. night owl, center of attention vs. behind the scenes, favorite holiday, a subject you want to learn more about, sports vs. fine arts, type A personality vs. easygoing, homebody vs. traveler, lived in same state whole life or in more than one, place in the family (youngest, middle, oldest), couch potato vs. busy bee, favorite way to relax. Be sure to make your bingo card with options that work well for your group. Everyone will use an identical copy of the same bingo card.

Directions: Invite participants to mingle and find a different person to answer and sign each of the squares on their bingo cards. Someone who completes a row or a column yells out "Bingo!" and introduces to the whole group the people who signed the card and their unique characteristics.

Wrap-up: Strengths come in different packages. Diversity makes life interesting and reflects multiple ways in which we are unique and different.
- What did you learn about each other from this activity?
- What does this activity say about the importance of relationships?
- How do our misperceptions of diversity prevent us from understanding and getting to know each other?
- What do we do in our programs and in our team to encourage a mutual respect?

Key Elements: Celebration, Community Building, Communication, Working Together

Asset Categories: Support, Positive Identity, Social Competencies, Empowerment, Commitment to Learning

LISTENING CONCENTRIC CIRCLES

Purpose: To help participants explore the importance of active listening as a key strategy of effective teamwork and youth work; to introduce healthy parameters for creating a safe space for listening and sharing

Estimated Time: 6–10 minutes

Supplies: None

Directions: Form two teams by asking the group to number off into ones and twos. Ask the ones to form a circle, facing outward. Have the twos surround them with a circle, facing inward. Spacing should be such that people face each other in pairs. If you have an odd number of people, simply let one pair include a third person.

Instruct participants to introduce themselves to their partners on your signal, at which point they will have one minute to talk about the question you provide. You will let them know when the time is halfway up and it is the second person's turn to talk. (Use whatever signal you want to alert them when time is up—call out "switch," blow a train whistle, etc.)

When time is up, instruct one of the circles to rotate (for example, the inner circle moves one person to the left) while the other circle stays still. This will give each person a new partner. Announce a new question and repeat the process.

Partner Questions:
- When is the last time you remember being fully listened to? How did it feel?
- What made that person a good listener?
- What may make it hard for you to really listen?
- What can you do to become a better listener?
- How can you practice listening on your job?

Option 2: Let pairs go through a series of deeper questions together instead of rotating. Set enough time so that each person is given equal opportunity to share. Instruct the listeners not to interrupt, but to focus attentively, their full attention on the speakers.

Option 2 Questions:
- Some strong feelings I've been having about work lately are . . .
- Some strong feelings I've been having about issues facing our youth are . . .
- A high point of working with youth this week has been . . .
- A place of peace for me is . . .
- Something that keeps me grounded for this work is . . .

Wrap-up:
- How can listening play a key role in conflict resolution?
- In clear communication and understanding others?
- In creative problem solving?
- How do listeners sometimes abuse the trust given them to listen and hear someone out? How do we sometimes frustrate the person who wants us to listen?
- On the flip side, how can listening play an important role in creating space for self-discovery?

Everyone deserves the respect and gift of being listened to. In youth and community development work, adults often find themselves playing many roles, such as counselors, referees, and guides. Sometimes those roles call for quick decisions, solving issues, fixing problems, or stepping in. Sometimes, though, people simply need to be heard and respected. There are times when people need the time and space to listen to and hear their own voices, out loud, in the presence of another caring person, in order to figure out what they really think and believe. That requires us to work at not fixing, interrupting, solving, analyzing, saving, or even trying to relate by sharing our own stories ("I remember when the exact same thing happened to me . . ."). And it may require us to work to maintain trust and not share what was said with anyone.

What will you remember about this activity that you will use?

Key Elements: Communication, Working Together, Vision, Conflict Resolution, Creative Problem Solving, Community Building

Asset Categories: Support, Social Competencies, Positive Values, Boundaries and Expectations

Partner questions contributed by Louisa Avery, Nashville, Tennessee

TRUE HEADINGS

Purpose: To help participants explore group strengths and preferences, and how they affect group work

Estimated Time: 15–25 minutes

Supplies: Four signs with one direction on each sign:
North: Let's go! Likes to do, act, try things, plunge in . . .
West: Let me map it out first. Likes to know all the details before acting.
East: Let me get a sense of where we are. Likes to look at the big picture before acting.
South: Is everyone good? Likes to know that everyone's feelings have been considered, everyone's voice has been heard, and all are invested and ready to go.

Copies of the discussion questions below for each group.

Directions: Invite participants to stand by the sign with the navigational direction, or heading, of their choice—the one that most closely matches who they are, not who they would like to be or want to be. Then ask each of the four groups to discuss the following questions, with one person in each group taking notes.

Inform groups that they will be asked to share some of what they have discussed with the larger group after 12–15 minutes of discussion.

Discussion Questions:

1. What does this direction mean to you? Why did you choose it? What are our particular strengths? What are our shortcomings?
2. Does the distribution of people among the different directions mean anything? Why are people where they are? Does the distribution have anything to do with the type of work that people are in?
3. When it comes to groups (any groups—youth groups, work teams, clubs, etc.), what is the best combination of "directional strengths" for a group to have? Should it be balanced? Does a group need more of one strength than another? Does it matter?
4. What is something about each of the other directions that drives people in our direction crazy?
5. What is something our group appreciates about each of the other directions? What strengths do they have that we admire?
6. How do their strengths complement our shortcomings? How do we complement them?

Wrap-up: Navigation is an important aspect in travel—knowing directions, taking the best route. As we apply that metaphor to life, it is equally important to know the directional bents of our group—who to call on for particular tasks based on strengths and interests, as well as how to navigate messy terrain when directions seem to conflict.

- What can we do to avoid being driven crazy by opposing directions? How can we safeguard against that? How can we deal with our "directional opposites" in a healthy way?
- What is the importance of this exercise for all of us as a team?
- What do we want to remember about this particular activity? What will we take from it?

Key Elements: Communication, Working Together, Conflict Resolution, Creative Problem Solving

Asset Categories: Support, Positive Identity, Social Competencies, Empowerment, Boundaries and Expectations

Insider's Tip: This activity facilitates self-discovery for the group and allows participants to express personalities and communication preferences in a fun, easy manner. At the same time, it pushes them to think more deeply about their colleagues—who they are, how they communicate, and how best to work together during personality and communication snags.

Developed in the field by educators affiliated with the National School Reform Faculty. Adapted with permission from www.nsrfharmony.org.

STRONG SUITS

Purpose: To allow participants time to explore their personal strengths and how they can best build young people's strengths based on who those young people are

Estimated Time: 15–20 minutes

Supplies: Copies of the "Strong Suits Leadership Styles" chart

Directions: Ask participants to review the chart and ponder these questions: "What are your greatest strengths in leadership? What are your special natural abilities, the recurring patterns that dominate your behavior?" Using the column on the right, mark your top leadership style(s). Identify one action point you will take based on your leadership style. For example, if you are a creator and have been thinking about an idea you'd like to try at work, perhaps you will outline your idea and share it with three people in the next 60 days.

Find a partner and talk about your strengths using the guiding questions. Discuss together how you can/do utilize your own strengths to better your team. How can you have an impact on others?

Wrap-up: Ask all participants to talk about their primary leadership style(s) and how they might be an asset to the team.

- How do we use our strengths and natural gifts to help shape the youth we know and work with?
- How do we make a difference for them by simply being the best "us" we can be?
- How can we encourage youth and adults in their natural leadership styles?

Remind the group of the importance of knowing our strengths and using them to maximize our personal influence and our contributions to our teams and community work.

Key Elements: Communication, Working Together, Community Building, Vision, Celebration

Asset Categories: Support, Positive Identity, Social Competencies, Empowerment, Boundaries and Expectations, Positive Values

Strong Suits Leadership Styles

LEADERSHIP STYLE	DESCRIPTION	NOTES: ME AND MY TEAM
DREAMER	You constantly think of new ideas and new ways to do things. You see potential in people and organizations, so you often ask, "How can I transform this from average to excellent?"	
CREATOR	You like to create and build new things. You are good at looking at a blank page and seeing wonderful designs and mapping out functional systems.	
PLANNER	You love organizing, numbers, calendars, and details. You are able to see through clutter and find the best patterns. You easily evaluate alternative scenarios to choose the best route for success.	
NETWORKER	You love bringing people together. You have a knack for seeing people's strengths and introducing them to people who need their talents. When you hear of a need, you are quick to connect them to resources.	
MOTIVATOR	You have a knack for getting people excited about things, making everything sound fun and inviting. You like to tell stories, make jokes, play games—anything to bring energy to the task at hand! With your enthusiasm, you are a great recruiter.	
ARRANGER	You are decisive, confident, purposeful, adventurous, bold, and action-oriented. You are a natural conductor, and you enjoy arranging multiple tasks to make things efficient and productive.	
CARETAKER	You can sense the emotions of those around you, and you intuitively see the world through their eyes and share their perspective. Relationships are important to you, and you want to make sure everyone is included.	
CELEBRATOR	You naturally look for moments to celebrate. You like to applaud people, successes, events, and progress. You are known for sending thank-you notes and remembering birthdays, anniversaries, and other key dates.	

WALK AND TALK

Purpose: To encourage dialogue and reflection on issues that are important to the group, and to engage different voices and perspectives to deepen understanding of the issue at hand

Estimated Time: 30 minutes

Supplies: Chart paper, markers

Directions: Provide a discussion topic, or ask the group to determine a topic they wish to discuss (for example, a current issue in youth work).

After a topic is selected, have participants find partners so that everyone is in pairs. If there are an odd number of people, one group can be a trio. Give them 15 minutes to talk about the topic together. If space and time permit, let pairs walk as they talk or find a space of their choice for their conversation.

When time is up, ask each pair to take 5 minutes to reflect on their conversation and to choose two major insights—facts, statements, questions, things they are curious about—to share with the big group. Their task is to articulate two things that stood out to them and to offer others a glimpse into how they processed and thought about the subject.

As the groups share their insights, record them on chart paper. Finally, lead a general discussion about what people said, the insights they shared, emerging themes, considerations for work, new ideas, or possibilities.

Wrap-up: Thank everyone for their hard work and valuable input. As required by the foregoing conversation, follow up with appropriate action steps, further conversations, and so on.

Key Elements: Communication, Working Together, Team Building, Vision, Creative Problem Solving, Conflict Resolution

Asset Categories: Support, Empowerment, Commitment to Learning, Boundaries and Expectations, Social Competencies, Positive Values

Insider's Tip: This activity provides a safe way to engage all participants and get their take on issues facing youth, the community, or a program/agency. It lets each person have a voice and sets an expectation for the groups to listen to each other and share what is important to them in a nonthreatening manner.

EXPLORING PERSPECTIVES AND VIEWPOINTS

Purpose: To encourage input on complex issues from as many different voices as possible for a fuller perspective, clarity, and understanding about what needs to be done

Estimated Time: 70–90 minutes

Supplies: Chart paper, markers

Note: This activity works best for a maximum of eight people. If teams are larger, split them into smaller groups and run the same process for the smaller groups in different rooms before bringing them back together for a summary discussion (8–10 minutes) before step four.

Directions: Tell participants that the purpose of this activity is to understand an issue and each other's perspectives more fully, not to find the "right" answer. Ask them to agree to a simple covenant:

- No side conversations
- No criticizing or put-downs
- All participants have a chance to speak if they wish
- Ask curious questions

Finally, and most importantly, there is the conversation rule: *no fixing, no saving, no advising, no setting anyone straight.*[1] Working with this rule opens up possibilities by counteracting the tendency to shut things down by looking for answers and being in "expert mode." It allows us to go deeper and uncover layers of a story or an issue that are not readily accessible when we focus on quick fixes or answers.

The Start: Double Team
Announce the topic to be discussed (for example, youth on boards, where our agency should focus energy and vision during difficult economic times, habits of effective groups, the next program endeavors we should take on). Ask participants to pair up and talk about the topic for 12 minutes.

Step 2: Three Major Insights
When time is up, give each pair chart paper and a marker. Tell participants they have 3 minutes to reflect on their conversations and to record on chart paper three major insights—facts, statements, questions—from their discussions. The goal is simply to share the most important parts of their conversations with the group.

Step 3: Overhearing
Pull everyone back together into a big group. Invite one pair to take 2–3 min-

---

[1]A countercultural rule used and practiced in Parker Palmer's work through the Center for Courage and Renewal and used by Richard L. Hester and Kelli Walker-Jones in their work in clergy leadership.

utes to share their three insights while the rest of the group listens, then give the group 5 minutes to discuss among themselves (not talking to the pair but to each other) what they heard. The presenting pair now listens. The group shares what they "overheard" the pair saying, how it resonates with them, and what it means to them. As participants talk to each other, they can summarize, ask questions, say what they are curious about, or share thoughts or experiences that echo, support, or differ from the major insights presented by the pair. Remind them of the covenant introduced at the beginning of the activity. The goal is to focus on the issue. After the 5-minute group dialogue, the presenting pair responds by taking 2 minutes to reflect aloud on what they heard from the group and to make their final comments. Repeat the 9–10-minute process for each pair.

Step 4: Review Insights
Point out the original lists of insights from the groups and lead a general discussion (10–15 minutes) covering everything that was shared.

Are there themes that connect all the lists? Has anyone had an "aha" moment as she thought about the subject and listened to everyone? Have new ideas or understandings emerged? Does anyone have a greater sense of clarity or a new perspective?

Note: The intent of this activity is to help participants gain a greater sense of clarity and perspective on a given issue. The activity can end at this point, leaving the group in a reflective mode with appropriate wrap-up comments asking what people will remember about this activity. Or, if needed, take a break and then distinctly move into a planning time using the following step.

Step 5: What's Next?
Based on what emerges from the process, determine the next steps that need to be taken in order to "give feet" to what was discussed. Does a covenant of understanding of how the group works together need to be documented? Does an action plan need to be outlined with who does what? Does a report need to be generated to educate others?

Wrap-up: Ask the group what they thought of the process as a method for including everyone's voice. Ask how the process worked for them as individuals. Thank them for their hard work and valuable input.

Key Elements: Communication, Working Together, Team Building, Vision, Creative Problem Solving, Conflict Resolution

Asset Categories: Support, Empowerment, Commitment to Learning, Boundaries and Expectations, Social Competencies, Positive Values

Insider's Tip: This activity comprises a progressive series of steps that divide thinking about an issue into smaller parts that are shared group by group for an overall general discussion and richer perspective. It is a good activity for engaging the whole group and getting everyone's input, expertise, perspective, and experience.

SENTENCE PUZZLES

Purpose: To illustrate that each person is needed to bring meaning and purpose to work; each holds a piece of the puzzle, and it takes all the pieces to make the whole

Estimated Time: 15–20 minutes

Supplies: 25 envelopes, each filled with four to six word cards

Preparation: Write one word on each card, five copies of each word, creating sets based on the following:

Envelope set #1: The, of, are, against
Envelope set #2: roared, ran, full, blessing, lapped, the
Envelope set #3: Forests, lion, real, Ocean
Envelope set #4: Friendships, dogs, trees, waves
Envelope set #5: The, quickly, are, a, shore

Facilitator Key: The goal is simply to make meaningful sentences. Some possibilities:

- The dogs ran quickly.
- Forests are full of trees.
- The lion roared.
- Friendships are a real blessing.
- Ocean waves lapped against the shore.

Directions: Divide the group into five teams of six or fewer; each group appoints one person to be its taskmaster. The taskmasters' job is to keep track of what happens during the activity (what they observe) *and* to make sure the people on their teams abide by the rules.

Give each group a set of five envelopes. Instruct the groups to open their envelopes and direct them to construct five meaningful sentences. Each person on the team must construct a sentence. The first word of each sentence is capitalized. That's your giveaway clue. Your team is done when each person has constructed a complete, meaningful sentence. There is no speaking. Exchanging of word cards is allowed but only through offering of cards, not by asking.

The taskmaster observes. The taskmaster does not direct, assist, or make suggestions. The taskmaster makes sure that there is no talking and that no one asks for word cards (by voice, clearing throats, raised eyebrows, signals, etc.). If anyone violates the rules, the taskmaster stops play. When the taskmaster determines that the team has constructed five intelligible, meaningful sentences, he calls "done."

Stop the game after the first team finishes.

Wrap-up:
- What was the task like?
- What made it difficult?
- How did you work around the challenge of not being able to talk?

- How is this activity an analogy for teamwork?
- How is this activity an analogy for community?

Sometimes our work with youth can feel like being presented with the envelopes—we get pieces of what's going on in their lives. Sometimes it may feel like certain things are missing from their lives and we're working a little harder to help make their lives meaningful—just like how we took the words and had to discover meaning within them.

The good news is that each young person does indeed have something to build from. We're not working from scratch. All children and youth have strengths and abilities. With help from the assets, we can enrich what they have and help piece together value for their lives.

Key Elements: Communication, Working Together, Creative Problem Solving, Community Building

Asset Categories: Support, Boundaries and Expectations, Empowerment, Commitment to Learning

Developed in the field by educators affiliated with the National School Reform Faculty Adapted with permission from www.nsrfharmony.org

MISSED SIGNALS

Purpose: To illustrate the importance of listening, asking curious questions, and being intentional in conversations for the purpose of creating understanding and not making assumptions

Estimated Time: 8–12 minutes

Supplies: List of the 40 Developmental Assets (see page 12)

Directions: Read aloud the following excerpt from *Pictures of Hollis Woods* by Patricia Reilly Giff.

> *This picture has a dollop of peanut butter on one edge, a smear of grape jelly on the other, and an X across the whole thing. I cut it out of a magazine for homework when I was six years old. "Look for words that begin with W," my teacher, Mrs. Evans, had said.*
>
> *She was the one who marked in the X, spoiling my picture. She pointed. "This is a picture of a family, Hollis. A mother, M, a father, F, a brother, B, a sister, S. They're standing in front of their house, H. I don't see one W word here."*
>
> *I opened my mouth to say: How about W for wish, or W for want, or W for "Wouldn't it be loverly," like the song the music teacher had taught us?*
>
> *But Mrs. Evans was at the next table by that time, shushing me over her shoulder.*

Ask the group for their general impressions of this story. What stands out to them?

Wrap-up:
- How is the story a narrative of our work with youth? How are we like Mrs. Evans? How are our youth like the youth in the story?
- Ask the group to show by raised hands how many have ever missed an opportunity or a cue to engage more deeply with a young person.
- At its core, what is the story about?
- What would have given this story a different ending?

Note that this story has some holes in it. Mrs. Evans missed an opportunity to have a dialogue with and listen to the young person, to ask curious questions, and to engage the youth in a conversation to find out what was going on in her head. Instead, she assumed what was going on or not going on. With attention and intentionality, the holes could have been filled easily.

There are holes in the development of youth that can be filled through their relationships with us. The list of assets gives us concrete things we can do and build to fill in the holes.

- Which assets are missing from the lives of the youth you know?
- How can you engage in a conversation with them to deepen your understanding of which assets they have and which ones they need? How can you use this list to avoid missing opportunities to create a deeper relationship?

Key Elements: Communication, Vision

Asset Categories: Support, Social Competencies, Boundaries and Expectations, Positive Values

Insider's Tip: This activity is an opener. It is an easy "thought for the day" that can be shared, pondered silently, and then discussed within a group as a reflective exercise.

Activity originally developed by Debbie Bambino
Adapted with permission from www.nsrfharmony.org

THE POWER IN MY HANDS

Purpose: To help participants think about their roles as positive, caring examples for young people

Estimated Time: 10–12 minutes

Supplies: Colored or white paper; markers, pencils, or pens

Directions: Ask participants to trace their hands on the paper and label each finger using the following criteria:
- Thumb: a unique gift/asset that you share with youth
- Index finger: a point you want to remember from today or a message you hope to communicate with the youth in your life
- Middle finger: a goal related to positive youth development that you have set for yourself
- Ring finger: a person in your life with whom you want to make more effort to connect
- Pinky finger: a value you want to wrap around all you do
- Palm: what keeps you going; your passion

After completing their hands, participants find partners, shake hands, and discuss the power they carry.

Wrap-up: Ask for volunteers to share some of their comments with the whole group.
Talk about the value of the power in their hands:
- Look at the unique gift or strength you wrote on your thumb. Just as you use your thumbs throughout the day, remember to share your gifts with young people consistently, every day.
- Let your index finger remind you of that key thing that is important to you.

- Look at the goal you wrote on your middle finger. When you look at your longest finger, remember to reach for the goals you've set for yourself.
- Let your ring finger remind you of the relationships in your life, and remind you to be intentional in your efforts to connect with the person you identified.
- Let your pinky finger remind you to keep your words and actions "wrapped around" the values that are important to you.
- Let your palm remind you of your "lifeline" and your passion. Be purposeful about keeping your passions as an integral part of your life.

You carry your hands with you everywhere you go. Within them is the power to share life with the people around you, to help shape them from your own goodness and vitality. Research tells us that having a caring adult role model is a vital factor in the lives of young people. Now your hands can serve as symbols to remind you to live vibrantly and purposefully. Go forth and live with intention to use your power to better the relationships around you.

Key Elements: Communication, Vision, Community Building

Asset Categories: Support, Social Competencies, Boundaries and Expectations, Positive Values

Activity contributed by Marilyn Peplau, New Richmond, Wisconsin

TOWER ASSETS

Purpose: To introduce the concept of asset building

Estimated Time: 15 minutes

Supplies: 40 wooden blocks (such as Jenga blocks), copies of the 40 Developmental Assets (see page 12), permanent marker

Preparation: Use the marker to label each of the 40 wooden blocks with one of the 40 Developmental Assets. Set up the blocks in a tower.

Directions: Challenge participants to take turns removing the blocks, one at a time, removing as many as they can without knocking down the tower.

When a block is pulled, talk about the asset written on that block. Read the definition, then ask the participant to share an example of how that asset can be nurtured in youth.

Tell the group the percentage of youth who said they have that particular asset in their lives. (You can find the percentages at www.search-institute.org/research/assets/assetfreq.)

After the tower falls down, note how many blocks were removed before the tower toppled. Compare that number to the average number of assets youth report having (18). Interesting fact: Coincidentally, most groups topple the tower after about 18 pieces have been pulled.

Ask the group for ideas on how to strengthen their own assets. Use the ones that were pulled out to start that conversation.

Wrap-up: "These are the 40 building blocks that researchers have found that all children and youth need in order to succeed. Research proves that the more assets children have, the more positive choices they will make, and the fewer assets children have, the more risky behaviors they will adopt. Do these 40 characteristics reflect what we want to see in our youth? Are there other characteristics that we want our youth to have?

Facilitator's Note: You can use this activity as an educational activity, or as a starting point for developing your own principles for youth work.

Variation: For a thrifty, low-prep version, distribute the asset list, have participants close their eyes and place a finger somewhere on the page, then discuss whatever assets their fingers land near.

Key Elements: Vision, Celebration, Community Building

Asset Categories: All

Activity features elements contributed by Cindy Lawrence, Nashville, Tennessee

PEOPLE, PLACES, THINGS

Purpose: To help participants explore their own youth and the resources and strengths they had that helped ground them

Estimated Time: 8–15 minutes

Supplies: None

Directions: Invite participants to think silently for a moment about a person, place, or activity that grounded them when they were growing up. Whom could they lean on, trust, and feel safe or loved with? Where in the community did they feel safe and enjoy being? What activity did they love and enjoy doing?

Give participants 1 minute of silent reflection to identify *one* of those key elements that helped ground them, then ask them to get out of their seats, mingle, and find a partner. The partners ask yes or no questions, first to determine if a memory is of a *person*, *place*, or *activity*, then to narrow in more specifically: a next-door neighbor, the town coffee shop, basketball.

As one partner zeroes in and guesses correctly the broad category, the other partner can talk about why the person, place, or activity was an important part of his youth.

After 4 or 5 minutes, the partners switch roles so that each has a chance to talk about a memory.

Wrap-up: How many recalled a relationship? It makes sense if many people did, because youth (and adults) are most affected by relationships. Having a web of strong, supportive relationships is essential for youth to succeed.

We are always searching, though often subconsciously, for the people and places that fill our lives with meaning and purpose, the people and places that make our lives feel "complete." These are the things that ground us. How are we grounding our youth? How are we showing up as the caring adults? How are we helping youth find a sense of meaning and purpose? How are we helping them discover their sparks, their true passions?

Apply it more immediately to the people around you. How do we support each other with care? How do we encourage each other to follow our passions? How can we help ground each other so that we are our best each day?

Key Elements: Communication, Celebration, Community Building

Asset Categories: Support, Constructive Use of Time, Positive Values, Commitment to Learning

ASSET CLUSTERS

Purpose: To encourage participants to tap into their own wisdom and beliefs regarding the Developmental Assets

Estimated Time: 10–12 minutes

Supplies: 8 sheets of 8½" × 11" paper, masking tape

Preparation: Make posters labeled with the broad categories of Developmental Assets: Support, Empowerment, Constructive Use of Time, Boundaries and Expectations, Commitment to Learning, Social Competencies, Positive Values, Positive Identity (or buy a set of asset posters from www.searchinstitutestore .org). Tape the posters around the room.

Directions: Ask that each participant read the posters and then stand by the one that means the most to him. Next, ask each group to talk about the asset they have chosen. Use the following questions to spark their conversation; you can share all of them all at once, or call them out over time:

What does the poster's message mean to them? Was that particular asset a solid part of their own lives when they were younger? Or was its absence the reason they value it so highly? Why do they think it is so vital? How does that asset fit with each person's picture of what is important for young people?

Wrap-up: After 5–7 minutes, go around the room and ask each group to share an insight or something that was said about their particular asset.

Follow up as needed to facilitate further dialogue or to pull out more insights. Stay curious.

Key Elements: Communication, Vision, Celebration, Community Building

Asset Categories: All

Activity inspired by Mary Ackerman, St. Paul, Minnesota

TRICK OR TREAT WITH THE ASSETS

Purpose: To encourage participants to tap into their own wisdom and beliefs regarding the Developmental Assets

Estimated Time: 15–20 minutes

Supplies: 8 sheets of 8½" × 11" paper, tape, Jenga blocks (or use slips of paper), trick-or-treat bags (or plain paper bags), index cards

Preparation: Make eight posters, each with one of the icons of the broad Developmental Assets categories: Support, Empowerment, Constructive Use of Time, Boundaries and Expectations, Commitment to Learning, Social Competencies, Positive Values, Positive Identity (the icons can be downloaded from www.search-institute.org/news-desk/image-library). Post the icons on the walls. Number the blocks (or slips of paper) from 1 to 40, and write on them the asset that corresponds to each number. Place all of the Support assets in one trick-or-treat bag, all of the Empowerment assets into another trick-or-treat bag, and so on. On index cards, write each broad asset category and its definition, one asset category for each index card, to make eight "asset cards."

Directions: Ask participants to pick an icon that speaks to them for whatever reason. What do they think the symbol is? Why is it important?

Instruct the participants to cluster with other people who picked that same icon and to share their thoughts about it.

Give each group an asset card to define the icon they picked. Then give them a trick-or-treat bag containing the specific assets that relate to the asset category they chose. Have them examine the details of their chosen asset. Invite them to take 10 minutes to discuss two things: Why are these assets a treat for youth? What is a trick they can come up with to remember them?

Wrap-up: Ask each group to share some of what they discussed and their tricks for remembering the assets' worth.

Variation: Still using the icons taped to the wall to provide a visual, break the group into smaller teams. Give each team a trick-or-treat bag with category-specific assets. Invite the small groups to look at their asset blocks or slips and try to identify a common pattern or theme. Once they think they have identified the common theme, they should send a runner to you, the facilitator, to ask for the asset card, the supporting theme or definition, that they believe captures their theme. The runner takes the card back to the group and reads it out loud to see if they successfully matched the definition with the specifics they had. If they feel they have correctly matched their assets to its correct category, they verify with you. If, after hearing the definition, they don't believe they were correct, they can send their runner back for their next guess.

When the groups have finished identifying their asset categories, talk about the importance of the various "treats" for children and ask each group to come up with a "trick" to remember them.

Key Elements: Communication, Vision, Celebration, Community Building, Creative Problem Solving

Asset Categories: All

Activity contributed by Marilyn Peplau, New Richmond, Wisconsin

SCRIBBLE SKETCHES

Purpose: To encourage participants to explore important aspects of youth development

Estimated Time: 10–30 minutes.

Supplies: Each team of four to six players will need five to seven large Post-it Notes, a pad of paper, a writing utensil, and a list of the 40 Developmental Assets

Directions: Divide the group into teams of four to six players and ask them to sit together at tables an equal distance from you, the facilitator. Distribute to each team five Post-it Notes and scrap paper for drawing. Ask the teams to quickly think of four or five characteristics that they hope to nurture in young people (compassion, respect, love for learning, etc.). If you have a small group of 5–15 people, have them think up the characteristics individually.

Each team writes one characteristic on each of its Post-it Notes and turns them all in to you. (Facilitator's note: If you need to make this activity shorter, use the list of 40 Developmental Assets from Search Institute to make characteristic cards ahead of time, by putting one asset on each Post-it Note. Find the list of assets on page 12.) Shuffle the cards.

Each team chooses one member to send to you to find out what he will be drawing. You secretly show all the team representatives one of the Post-it Notes with a characteristic that young people need in order to succeed.

Representatives then return to their tables to sketch an image to represent the characteristic as quickly as possible, trying to get their team members to guess what they are sketching. For example, if your card said "creativity," the artist might draw a paintbrush and a paint palette. The first group to correctly guess the characteristic on the card wins that round.

Post the characteristic card on the wall after each round is completed. Continue play, rotating artists from each team, until you run out of cards or time.

The group that wins the most rounds wins the game.

Wrap-up: Note all the characteristics on the wall. Compare the characteristics to the list of the assets. As you look at the list, do you think of anything you would add? Talk about the characteristics your group hopes to individually or collectively nurture in youth. Brainstorm two or three ideas for action steps that the group can take to help build those characteristics through their work and/or programs.

Note: This activity could also serve as a nice lead-in to writing a group mission statement or for setting group goals.

Key Elements: Communication, Working Together, Celebration

Asset Categories: All

TANDEM THINKING

Purpose: To identify the people and structures that help young people thrive

Estimated Time: 12–15 minutes

Supplies: For each person, one lined index card, a writing utensil, and a copy of the 40 Developmental Assets (see page 12)

Directions: Divide the group into teams of four players, and distribute an index card to each person. Ask participants to quickly think about something that added strength to their childhood or adolescence (Boy Scout troop, swim team, high expectations, family support, etc.) and write their answers in large letters at the top of their index cards and circle them.

Participants then pass their cards clockwise. The new cardholders read the cards and write down the first word they think of when they read the cards. For example, if the card reads "Boy Scout troop," the new cardholder might write "eagle" on the line below. Participants continue passing the cards clockwise until each circled word has three associated words beneath it. Then they give the cards to you, the facilitator.

Shuffle the cards and ask for a volunteer to come forward to get the group to guess the circled word on one of the cards without using any of the other words listed on the card. Each volunteer has 45 seconds to get the group to guess the word using gestures or words other than those listed on the card.

Wrap-up: After playing, distribute the clue cards on the tables to serve as a visual reminder of the earlier conversations and ask:
- Which of the things that helped you be strong when you were young also help youth be strong today?
- What other factors help youth have strong character?

Distribute the list of assets and inform the group that the handout is a list of research-based factors that are proven to help youth live strong, healthy, well-supported lives. Ask them to scan the list, and ask: Of all the things we talked about and the list you have now, which factors do you want to intentionally build for and with the youth you know?

Key Elements: Communication, Working Together, Vision, Celebration

Asset Categories: All

Insider's Tip: This activity could serve as a nice lead-in to writing a group mission statement or setting group goals.

QUICK THINKING

Purpose: To promote positive relationships and activities for young people

Estimated Time: 15 minutes

Supplies: Index cards, pens, list of the 40 Developmental Assets

Preparation: Make alphabet cards by writing one letter on each index card (or buy alphabet flash cards). Make thought-prompter cards by writing these teasers on another set of index cards:

- Books that every young person should read
- Influential people
- Recreational activities for young people
- Musical instruments
- Things associated with a playground
- Things associated with the kitchen
- Musical group (vocal or instrumental)
- Things associated with volunteering
- Places to volunteer
- Ways to make a difference
- Ways to use skills and talents
- Important values
- Family traditions
- Something to be proud of or something that makes me proud
- Ways to help others
- Ways to show others that you care
- Movies every young person should watch
- Somewhere every young person should go/visit
- Favorite way to spend time
- Something every young person should know how to do

Directions: Divide the group into teams of five to seven people. Each team sends a representative to the game table for the first round. Have one person draw an alphabet card and a prompter card and flip them both over. The team representatives should quickly think of something that connects the alphabet letter and the category. For example, the letter C and "books every young person should read" might yield the response *Charlotte's Web*. When the representatives think of an answer, they raise their hands. The first team to give a viable match wins a point. Teams then send up new representatives for the next round. Continue rotations until time is called. The team with the most points wins the game.

Wrap-up: This activity is a fun method to think about ways to promote positive relationships, self-image, and involvement.

- What other cards would you create to learn more about others?
- What helps you be strong?
- How do you help others have a strong character and values?

Distribute the list of assets and invite participants to identify key assets that they can focus on to build for and with youth and peers to help them be strong.

Key Elements: Communication, Working Together, Vision

Asset Categories: All

SHIELDS IN BATTLE

Purpose: To remind adults of the battlefield raging around young people *and* the power they have to protect young people

Estimated Time: 15–20 minutes

Supplies: 10 sheets of 8½" × 11" paper per group, 8 sheets of card stock per group, markers

Preparation: Write one Developmental Asset category on each sheet of card stock with a one-sentence description of that asset category (see page 12), so that each sheet of card stock represents a different asset category.

Directions: Ask for a volunteer to represent a typical teenager (you can pick any grade between 6 and 12 to personalize this activity for your audience). Have this person stand in the front of the room.

Ask participants to name influences in our society that put this young person and all young people at risk. What are some of the negative influences that bombard them or could potentially tempt them away from a healthy life? What are some of the negative influences that they have to avoid or navigate every day? Solicit ideas until you have at least 10.

Ask for 10 additional volunteers to join you at the front of the room. Give them each a sheet of paper and ask them to wad it up. On your count, have the people throw the wads of paper at the volunteer typical teenager, trying to hit him.

Ask the volunteer teenager:
- How did it feel to have all those negative factors coming your way?
- Were you hit?
- What did you think your chances for success were?
- What would have helped protect you from harm?

Collect the paper balls and return them to group members and ask them to stay close by.

Comment on the fact that this young person needs some reinforcements to ward off all these negative influences. Ask the group to name some of the people and activities that influence their lives in positive ways (parents, teachers, religious leaders, peers, neighbors, sports, art, church, etc). Ask for eight volunteers to come to the front to help protect the young person. Give the volunteers one sheet of card stock each. Ask them to arrange themselves in a protective circle around the volunteer teenager and instruct them to protect their young person to the best of their ability. Once they have arranged themselves to their liking, ask the people holding the paper wads to throw them at the young person again on a three count.

Ask the volunteer teenager:
- How did it feel to have all those negative factors coming your way this time?
- How was it different?
- What did you think your chances for success were?
- Were you hit?

Note: If the volunteer teenager was hit, acknowledge that some negative influences are persistent and slip through—that's reality. However, the chances of bouncing back and surviving are higher when youth are surrounded by support.

Wrap-up: Ask each protector to read the name of the asset category on her card and its description.

Say, "The assets are proven factors to help protect youth and to provide positive influences that result in youth having strong, healthy lives and making good choices. The more of the assets they have in their lives, the better off they are."

Thank all volunteers for their help and ask them to take their seats. Ask participants what they will remember about this activity tomorrow.

Variation

Purpose: To help participants visualize the effect of stress and negative forces on a person and how important protective factors and skills are.

Directions: Follow the same process but this time explain to participants that the paper wads represent things that stress them out or make them feel yucky. And, of course, you will ask the volunteer teenager how it felt to have all that stress and negativity coming his way. Ask if the volunteer was able to avoid any of the missiles.

The shields will represent some of the practices, people, and activities that keep people sane during times of chaos, trouble, and stress. Again, ask the volunteer teenager how it felt to have all that stress and negativity coming his way. Ask if he was able to avoid any of the missiles.

Wrap-up: As a group, discuss the difference between dealing with stress and negativity when there are active practices for preservation and care and when there are none.
- What stops us from taking better care of ourselves?
- How might our own self-care or lack thereof affect our work with others? How might it affect the young people we work with and know?
- How can we be protectors and not negativity enforcers on our team?
- How is this activity an illustration of the power of support and positive influences?
- How can we improve those supports and influences? How can we actively combat the negativity and stresses that may influence youth?

Key Elements: Conflict Resolution, Community Building

Asset Categories: Support, Boundaries and Expectations, Empowerment, Positive Identity

ASSET MATCHUPS

Purpose: To help participants become more familiar with the 40 Developmental Assets and how they are nurtured in young people

Estimated Time: 10 minutes

Supplies: Full list of 40 Developmental Assets from page 12 (one list for each person, plus one list to cut up and use for the activity)

Hint: To make the asset list easier to manipulate for this activity, consider using the copy machine's "zoom" feature to make bigger copies.

Preparation: Cut one copy of the assets list into slips, separating the definitions from the assets they define. Adjust the number of asset definitions and terms you cut based on the number of participants and/or the assets your group needs to focus on growing. Make sure that you have the correct term and definition matches for what you distribute.

Directions: Give each person one slip—either an asset or a definition. Instruct participants to mingle, introduce themselves, and ask each other what they would do to help a young person strengthen the asset or asset definition they have in their hands. (An alternative question for this activity might be "What would it look like if this asset were well developed in a young person's life?")

Challenge participants to try to find their match. The people with asset definitions are looking for the people who have their particular asset word match and vice versa.

Have participants continue to circulate, asking and answering the question, until all have found their match. Provide each person with a list of the assets at the end of the activity.

Wrap-up: Each asset addresses an important issue affecting our young people. We recognize asset building when we see it. When we take the time to think about how we can build assets, one at a time, we realize how easy it can be. Every day we can take small steps toward making the lives of our children and adolescents a little bit better.

Key Elements: Vision, Community Building, Communication, Working Together

Asset Categories: All

RESPECT AND UNDERSTANDING

PROFESSIONAL LINEUPS

Purpose: To realize and make use of the expertise represented by individuals in the group

Estimated Time: 8–10 minutes

Supplies: None

Directions: Invite participants to form a sequential line based on one of the following:
- Length of time working in this school/organization—longest to shortest amount of time
- Length of time working in the field of youth work/education—longest to shortest amount of time

Wrap-up:
- What did you learn about one another in this exercise?
- How can you make use of your new knowledge about your team members?
- How might your team grow stronger as you respect and make use of the diversity of knowledge and understanding represented in your group?

Key Elements: Communication, Working Together

Asset Categories: Support, Constructive Use of Time, Boundaries and Expectations, Positive Values, Positive Identity

Activity contributed by Flora Sanchez, Albuquerque, New Mexico

VALUABLE EXCHANGE

Purpose: To enhance teamwork by understanding individual strengths *or* to gather ideas for vision and planning

Estimated Time: 10–15 minutes

Supplies: Flip chart, marker, and tape (optional); three pieces of play money for each person

Preparation: Make play money by using green paper and clip art from a computer. Draw a circle in the middle of the front of the bill and leave it blank. Leave space in each corner to designate an amount. Across the top write or type in the group name, for example, "United States of _____" or "Nation of _____" (fill in the blank with the name of your group). Leave space for a participant to write his name underneath the circle on the bill. The following is an example of what a blank play money bill might look like:

Directions: Give participants three pieces of play money each. Ask them to write their responses to your questions in the blank space in the center of the bills.

For building a team that makes use of the strengths of team members, ask the group: "What is one way you bring 'wealth' to the group? You might consider valuable skills, ideas, beliefs, or contributions that you bring to the team. For example, Vonnie is optimistic or Benji plays the guitar." Give participants five minutes to ponder the wealth of who they are and to record the value of what they bring.

For vision and goal setting, ask the group: "What is something you've been eager for our group to try? What is something you have wanted forever to do? What would you like to see the program/agency address? Where would you like to see it go?" (For example, the program/agency might offer parenting classes, write curriculum, have youth on boards, start a staff bowling league, etc.). Give participants five minutes to record some of their favorite ideas.

When time is up, ask participants to take 1 minute to look at their three bills and designate a dollar amount to each wealth item. Which one is $20? Which one is $50? Which one is "priceless"? They should write the appropriate denomination in the corners of each bill and write their names in the blank space at the bottom of each bill.

Ask participants to mingle for a few minutes in order to share the information they recorded on their bills.

Wrap-up:
- How did you determine what was "priceless" for you?
- What are some of the ideas/resources that excited you the most, whether they were from your bills or someone else's?
- How might our group respond to hearing these priceless resources? Do we need to change the way we work together, or make plans based on any of our ideas?

We each have valuable resources to share with others. Be intentional about having the courage and the humility to share with and learn from one another as a daily habit. When we share from the wealth of who we are, we will all be richer.

Note: Make a point of capturing and keeping the ideas and resources your group shared for future use. You could keep the bills or make a spreadsheet to store the information more easily.

Key Elements: Communication, Team Building, Visionary, Celebration

Asset Categories: Empowerment, Support, Social Competencies, Positive Values

WINDOWS

Purpose: To further understand colleagues' motivations and learn to build more supportive relationships

Estimated Time: 15–20 minutes

Supplies: A copy of the Love Languages Reflection Page handout (see page 58) and a writing utensil for each participant; a flip chart and five markers

Preparation: On each of five pieces of flip chart paper, draw a window: a horizontal line and a vertical line through the middle, making a cross that divides the paper into four equal quadrants. In large letters, label each of the top left quadrants with one of the five love languages—"Words of Affirmation," "Quality Time," "Receiving Gifts," "Acts of Service," and "Physical Touch." Label each of the top right quadrants "names," leaving room for participants to write beneath the label. Label the bottom left quadrants "supportive actions," with room for participants to write below. Finally, label the bottom right quadrants "deflating actions," with room for participants to write below. Place the "windows" around the room.

Directions: Say to the group, "According to research done by Dr. Gary Chapman, everyone has one way that he or she primarily gives and receives love, and today we're going to explore our own 'love languages' and the impact they have on our work with youth and adults."

Give everyone a Love Languages Reflection Page. Ask participants to think about it for 2–3 minutes and then rank their love languages from 1 to 5 (1 = most favored; 5 = least favored), according to their personal style.

Point out the five windows around the room. Ask participants to stand in front of the window that reflects their primary love language and write their names in the top right pane.

Ask each "window group" to think of actions that support or strengthen people with that particular love language. Have the groups record their thoughts in the bottom left windowpanes.

Ask the "window groups" to think of actions that cause them to feel deflated or shut down or powerless and write them in the bottom right windowpanes. The actions might not affect people with other love languages at all, but they affect people with this love language in a negative way. Ask people to silently rotate among the windows, reading about each love language group, taking note of actions that support and deflate people with the various love languages.

Wrap-up:
- How does your primary love language affect your work relationships?
- Think of the youth and adults under your influence. What are their primary love languages?
- Do you need to alter the way you communicate compassion, based on their love language?
- Think of the colleague (or young person) with whom you have the most stressful relationship. How might love languages contribute to that stress? How might altering how you communicate based on each other's love language help with resolving conflicts?
- What action will you take today to make use of your knowledge of love languages?

Key Elements: Communication, Community Building, Conflict Resolution, Work-Life Balance

Asset Categories: Support, Social Competencies, Boundaries and Expectations

Adapted from research done by Dr. Gary Chapman
www.5lovelanguages.com

Love Languages Reflection Page

Rank the following love languages in accordance with your personal style, with 1 representing your most preferred love language and 5 being your least preferred love language.

_____ **Words of Affirmation**
- Likes to give and receive praise, encouragement, and compliments
- Dislikes hurtful words and deceit

_____ **Quality Time**
- Likes to give and receive undivided attention in conversation and activities
- Dislikes distractions or attempting to multitask while listening

_____ **Receiving Gifts**
- Likes to give and receive gifts—whether it's a flower or a gift certificate or an extravagant gift
- Dislikes thoughtless actions and forgotten moments

_____ **Acts of Service**
- Likes helpfulness—changing the computer toner or getting a cup of coffee or running errands
- Dislikes irresponsibility and laziness

_____ **Physical Touch**
- Likes to give and receive high fives, hugs, and pats on the back
- Dislikes isolation and inaccessibility

TEAM CONTINUUM DIALOGUE

Purpose: To help participants explore and share in a nonthreatening way their beliefs, perspectives, and values about themselves and their team

Estimated Time: 20–25 minutes

Supplies: None

Directions: Describe the process of a continuum dialogue to the group: You will read two opposite statements, and participants will place themselves somewhere on an imaginary arc between the statements. Designate one end of the arc for the first statement and the other end for the second statement. Read aloud one set of statements, and allow everyone to choose where to stand on the arc.

Once everyone has made a choice, ask for volunteers to share why they chose their positions. As with any group activity, participants should show respect, give full attention to the people who are talking, and not challenge or tease them. And, as people listen to and reflect on what's been said, they can change their minds and move to different positions. If they want to say why they moved, give them an opportunity to do so. Encourage participants to be honest and to consider what they are most likely to do on a daily basis rather than what they *think* they should do. After they have finished explaining their positions, read aloud another set of statements and again allow participants to find their places on the arc. Repeat as often as you wish.

Choose from the following options the continuum dialogue statements that best reflect issues your group needs to explore. After each choice is a question to discuss further. Use as desired.

Practice round:

(a) sweet

(b) salty

(a) I believe in "start on time/end on time." I am always on time.

(b) Watch? Who has a watch? Time doesn't mean anything.

What does time feel like to you? How does time affect your work?

(a) I am available 24/7.

(b) My work phone is off when I'm "off the clock" at work.

What does availability mean to you?

(a) My work space is neat and orderly; everything has its place.

(b) My work area looks like utter chaos and I love it!

What role does your work space play for you?

(a) I do my best work in the morning.

(b) I do my best work in the evening.

How do you balance time accordingly?

(a) I like a quiet and still environment.　(b) I enjoy a loud and busy environment.

What role does environment/space play in your work life?

(a) I am a multitasker.　(b) I prefer to be focused on one thing at a time.

What role does focus play for you in getting things done?

(a) I like free-flowing mind mapping.　(b) I like structured outlines.

How do these styles affect how we think together as a group?

(a) I need hard and fast deadlines to keep focused.　(b) I need flexible timelines to allow for freedom.

What roles do preferences and structure play in your work life?

(a) I prefer narrative and stories.　(b) I prefer lists and bullets.

What does communication mean to you?

(a) Tasks come first.　(b) Relationships are more important than tasks.

What roles do tasks and relationships play in your work life?

(a) I think best out loud with a group.　(b) I think best when I have quiet time to ponder and reflect.

What roles do people and spaces play in your best thinking?

(a) I am motivated primarily from within.　(b) I am motivated and energized primarily by others' leadership and vision.

What does motivation mean to you?

(a) I like to work alone.　(b) I'll work with anyone and everyone, the more the merrier.

How does the number of people you work with influence your ability to do good work?

(a) My personal space allows people within two inches.　(b) My personal space requires at least a two-foot distance.

What happens when people invade your personal space?

(a) I wear my emotions on my sleeve.　(b) I keep my emotions private and share with a select few.

What role do emotions play in your work life?

Wrap-up:

This process is great for digging deeper concerning what makes people tick and really learning about each other's styles and preferences.

- What new insights did you gain from this activity? What gave you food for thought?
- What potential application of what we've talked about do you see?
- How might your new understanding affect your work?
- What do you need to remember from this exercise?

Key Elements: Communication, Conflict Resolution, Creative Problem Solving, Work-Life Balance

Asset Categories: Support, Positive Values, Commitment to Learning, Empowerment, Boundaries and Expectations

Insider's Tip: This activity can be used to provide space for staff to hear each other out with respect on issues that revolve around the group and how they function as a group.

Adapted from the continuum dialogue developed by Marylyn Wentworth and expanded and enriched by many facilitators in the National School Reform Faculty, www.nsrfharmony.org. Used by permission.

INTERSECTIONS

Purpose: To help participants be aware of how they view and define themselves and be aware of the diversity of identities within a group—where people have shared spaces and where people have different identities

Estimated Time: 20–30 minutes

Supplies: None

Directions: Inform the group that you will be calling out several categories and asking them to group themselves by how they view each category. Say, "For example, if the word *education* were called out, people might form groups based on what?" Get a few quick answers on how they might form groups. Let them know that there is no right or wrong way of grouping. Call out one of the terms from the list below and let groups form:
- Geography
- Upbringing
- Birth order
- Money
- Response to change
- Role in program/agency
- Energy level
- Personality
- Outlook on life
- Technology

Once groups are formed, go around the room and ask each group to denote its organizing principle. Ask the groups to stay together and give them one of the following questions to discuss as a small group. Allow 3–5 minutes per question.
- What does it mean to you to be . . . ?
- How much do you define yourself by this descriptor?
- What does it mean to be this way versus the other descriptors present in the room?
- How is our group different from the other groups? How are we similar to the other groups?

- What is one thing you would like the other groupings to know about your particular group and what it means to be you?
- What is one thing you appreciate about the other groupings in the room that are different from you?

Ask groups to share the key points of what they talked about within their small groups.

Call out a new grouping, and repeat the process.

Wrap-up:
- Did anyone change his or her interpretation based on how other people defined a category?
- What role does self-identity play in how we engage with each other and with young people?
- How is knowing a person's story key to better understanding and respect?
- What do we do to actively build common understanding and respect within our group?

Key Elements: Communication, Team Building, Community Building, Conflict Resolution

Asset Categories: Social Competencies, Positive Identity, Support

Insider's Tip: This activity examines diversity from various angles and helps participants explore their own self-identity. It also provides a backdrop from which participants can then think about how they are similar to and different from young people today. This awareness can help equip participants to engage with each other (or the youth they work with) in finding common ground while also respecting differences of experiences.

Developed in the field by educators affiliated with the National School Reform Faculty Adapted with permission from www.nsrfharmony.org

SPARKS SPEEDY CONVERSATIONS

Purpose: To give participants an opportunity to explore their interests and passions

Estimated Time: 10–20 minutes

Supplies: A watch or timer to measure minutes and seconds

Directions: Ask the group to stand in two lines, facing each other, spaced so that pairs are formed. For groups with an odd number of people, simply let one pair include a third member.

Tell participants that they are participating in a form of Speedy Conversations—"speed dating," if you will. To that end, each pair will have 1½ minutes to introduce themselves to each other and talk about the question you will call out. You will let them know (call out "switch," blow a train whistle, etc.) when 45 seconds have passed and it is time for the second person to talk.

When time is up, instruct one of the lines to move sideways so that there are new pairs. For example, ask one line to move one person to the left; the person at the end will go all the way to the other end of the line. Repeat for as many conversation rounds as you wish.

The questions relate to the idea that everyone has one or more "sparks": something that gives your life meaning and purpose—an interest, a passion, or a gift.

Sparks Questions (in no particular order)
- What makes your eyes light up with joy?
- What makes you laugh out loud?
- When do you feel most alive?
- What gives you energy?
- What could you talk about forever?
- What makes your heart smile most warmly?
- What fuels your passion for your (youth) work?
- What's your favorite quote/motto to live by?
- What's your favorite quote related to youth work?
- What screen saver would best describe your interests?
- What were your sparks when you were a young person? What are they today?
- Who nurtured your sparks?
- How are you pursuing your sparks? What room do you make for them in your life?
- How does/might pursuing your sparks affect your career and your personal life?

Wrap-up:
- Why do you think it might be important to know your own spark(s)?
- Why might it be important to nurture sparks in ourselves, with each other, and with the young people we know?
- What impact do sparks have on how we live our lives?
- How does knowing our sparks affect the impact we wish to have on others?

Key Elements: Communication, Vision, Celebration, Community Building, Inspiration, Work-Life Balance

Asset Categories: Support, Empowerment, Constructive Use of Time, Positive Identity

Insider's Tip: This activity provokes thought about participants' own lives and what makes them tick, and it allows them to engage in an exploratory conversation about things that they probably don't already know. To explore more research on sparks, visit www.ignitesparks.com.

PAPER AMY

Purpose: To remind participants of the importance of a supportive, encouraging environment for youth and how we can use our words to have a powerful positive or negative impact on a person

Estimated Time: 5–10 minutes

Supplies: Paper plate and marker

Preparation: Draw a smiley face in the middle of a paper plate and give "Amy" some curly hair.

Directions: Give the group a story or scenario similar to the following:

This is my 12-year-old friend Amy. (Hold up the paper plate with the smiley face on it.) *Like every young person, Amy should have the opportunity to feel loved and capable and be encouraged by others. Unfortunately, on any given day that's not typically what happens. Here's how a day goes:*

- *Amy gets up late and throws on whatever clothes are lying around her room. She gets on the bus, and one of the other children starts snickering and pointing at her holey tennis shoes and mix-matched clothes.* (Rip off a piece of Amy.)

- *As Amy gets to school, she rushes to get off the bus and away from the girl who teased her about her shoes. She leaves in such a rush that she forgets her math book and has to run back to get it. The principal sees her hustling into school right before the bell rings and says, "Almost late again, Amy. I suppose I'll be seeing you in my office later, if this is any sign of how your day is going to go."* (Rip off a piece of Amy.)

- *Amy runs down the hall trying to get into her classroom on time and trips over her shoelaces, falling down in the hall. Other children point and laugh: "Look at Amy! She's such a klutz!"* (Rip off a piece of Amy.)

- *Amy, red faced, gets to her seat and sits down. Her neighbor, Jill, tells her that she's not talking to Amy today because she saw her talking to that new girl, Trish, and that she hasn't decided if Trish is okay or not. So if Amy is going to be friends with Trish, then she can't be friends with Jill.* (Rip off a piece of Amy.)

- *Amy is feeling really low. Her clothes are rumpled, her shoes aren't right, the principal doesn't believe in her, she's a klutz, and now Jill is mad at her just because she was nice to a new student.* (Rip off a piece of Amy.) *She thinks to herself, "What's wrong with me that others have to pick at me and don't see anything good in me? I must be stupid or something."* (Rip off a piece of Amy.)

Wrap-up:
The words we say affect others greatly. Amy is all torn up. It will take a lot of work to put Amy back together. It can be done, but it takes extra effort—time, nice words, sincere compliments, encouragement, and, of course, tape, for Paper Amy. Even with all the work, Paper Amy will *still* have little cracks that will be sensitive to certain comments; she won't be as whole as if none of the unkind words, teasing, and bullying had taken place.

- How might Amy's day have been made better? What could have been said or could be said now to make Amy whole?
- What could the people Amy encountered have done differently to have a positive impact on her?
- What could Amy do to make herself stronger and more resistant to negative factors?
- What strategy can we adopt to ensure that we make supporting and encouraging youth a priority for our work? For our community? What will help us remember to give priority to this too little valued aspect of positive youth development?

Key Elements: Communication, Community Building

Asset Categories: Support, Boundaries and Expectations, Social Competencies

Insider's Tip: Change the story to fit the needs or interests of your audience; for example, "Amy" can become "Tom," the school setting can become a neighborhood, the rural town can became an urban environment. This activity pairs well with Four-Letter Words (see below).

Adapted from an activity by Julie Stevens, Gahanna, Ohio

FOUR-LETTER WORDS

Purpose: To illustrate the importance of words for praise, communication, and conflict resolution

Estimated Time: 10–15 minutes

Supplies: Alphabet flash cards (one pack for every 28 participants)

Preparation: Check to see if your alphabet cards have blank cards that can be used as wild cards. If there are no blank cards, create two or three of your own wild cards with index cards marked by a star.

Directions: Show the group a wild card, and explain that it can represent any letter. Distribute one card to each player. Ask players to mingle and create groups of four with whom they can make "G-rated" four-letter words (no profanities).

Once a group forms a word, have them stand together, spelling their word with letters held in front of them. Call time at 30 seconds and ask volunteers to share their words. Play additional rounds, encouraging players to form words with new partners each time.

When you are finished, have participants circle up or sit down as you talk about the game. Collect all the cards.

State, "This was a simple game. On the surface, it is about knowing your ABCs and forming words. However, it specifically dealt with four-letter words."

- What do four-letter words have to do with the workplace?
- What is the equivalent of four-letter words in the workplace? How do unkind words show up on a day-to-day basis?
- What is the importance of "G-rated words" in the workplace, with our team or with youth?
- What power do words have? How can words communicate what we feel, believe, and think? How can words help inspire or generate a sense of vision and community?
- How can words help us resolve conflicts peacefully and promote understanding?

Say, "Besides illustrating that words can hurt or heal, this game also highlights the importance of every letter."

- How did it feel to be a vowel? A rarely used letter? A wild card? How did it feel to be a Q? What did Q need?
- What might this game say about how we are a community together?
- How can we honor each other with our diverse skills, backgrounds, and personalities without expecting a V to act like a T or an R to behave like an E?

Wrap-up: This game reminds us that non-G-rated four-letter words—and also gossip, making unfair assumptions, and spreading rumors—have no place in the kind of community we hope to create. It also reminds us that all the letters are needed: all gifts are needed, and no gift is more valuable than another.

Key Elements: Communication, Working Together, Conflict Resolution, Team Building

Asset Categories: Support, Social Competencies, Positive Identity

Adapted from Great Group Games *by Susan Ragsdale and Ann Saylor*

TWIRLS AND SWIRLS

Purpose: To help adults realize the importance of creating transitions in youth programming, and to help them recognize the emotions and thoughts swirling in the minds of youth and how they affect a young person's functioning

Estimated Time: 5–10 minutes

Supplies: None

Directions: Ask participants to write their names in the air with imaginary pens.

Ask the group: "Was that an easy task?" Respond to the group: "You did a good job. You achieved your task and you should feel a sense of success." Now ask everyone to cross one leg over the other and begin to twirl the extended foot in a clockwise direction. State, "The whirling is symbolic of all the thoughts and feelings people have whirling in their heads and hearts—at home, in the office, at school, in relationships, and so on." Next, instruct them to continue to whirl their feet around while they write their names in the air again.

Wrap-up: How well did you do in your attempt to whirl your foot and write simultaneously? It was much harder to do both, wasn't it? Likewise, it's sometimes difficult for young people to manage the whirling in their hearts and minds while simultaneously achieving tasks in school and extracurricular activities.
- How can we help youth make the transition from all the stuff that whirls in their heads to be more fully and capably present with our group?
- How can we calm transitions and help them focus?
- How can we help with that whirling in head and heart?

Key Elements: Communication, Community Building

Asset Categories: Support, Social Competencies, Boundaries and Expectations

Activity contributed by Marilyn Peplau, New Richmond, Wisconsin

WHAT SHAPE ARE YOU IN?

Purpose: To help participants be aware of the dynamics of their group as they work together

Estimated Time: 10 minutes

Supplies: Bendable items such as thin moldable wire, molding clay, Bendaroos, or pipe cleaners (long or regular size)—one per person

Directions: Give each person a pipe cleaner (or whatever moldable object you are using). Form the group into teams of four to six participants. Ask participants to create sculptures to reflect their answers to this question: "What shape do you feel like you are in as we begin this meeting?" Have team members introduce themselves to each other, sharing their sculptures and comments.

Wrap-up:
- Why is it important for us to be sensitive to the shape we're in? To the shape our teammates are in?
- How can sensitivity, understanding, and support strengthen our team?

It's important as we face our vision and our work each day to know what shape we are in, to offer ourselves grace, and to give the best that we can give from the time, energy, and inner strength that we have today. It is also important to know what shape we are in for the sake of asking for support and help when we need it, and to be a support for our teammates when they need help and support.

Key Elements: Communication, Community Building

Asset Categories: Support, Commitment to Learning, Boundaries and Expectations

WISDOM OF THE WOODCUTTER

Purpose: To illustrate the importance of self-care in youth work

Estimated Time: 8–12 minutes

Supplies: List of the 40 Developmental Assets

Directions: Share the following story:
Once upon a time, there was a very strong woodcutter. He was the fastest, strongest woodcutter around. He was hired on the first day and fired on the fourth day. Why? The first day he cut down 40 trees. The second day he brought down 25 trees. The third day he toppled 20 trees, and on the fourth, he cut down 10. When he was fired, the woodcutter asked, "Why? I worked hard, I took no breaks, I was always working . . ." The manager replied: "That may be, but you never took the time to sharpen your blade."

Wrap-up:
The moral of the story? You have to take time to sharpen your blade. When we are working with youth, we often pour ourselves into the work. However, if we pay no attention to ourselves and don't take care of ourselves, we might very well lose our ability to stay sharp. If that happens, we might lose our effectiveness with the very people we want to help become healthy and thriving!
- What are some ways that you refuel your own emotional/physical/spiritual tank?
- What helps you stay sharp?
- What tips would you share with others to help them maintain balance in this work?
- Which assets aid you in your own health and development?

Key Elements: Communication, Work-Life Balance

Asset Categories: Support, Constructive Use of Time, Boundaries and Expectations, Positive Values, Positive Identity

Insider's Tip: This activity is an opener. It is an easy "thought for the day" that can be shared, pondered silently, and then discussed within a group as a reflective exercise.

ROAD SIGNS

Purpose: To help participants reflect on their lives and how they have shaped who they are today

Estimated Time: 50–60 minutes

Supplies: Paper, colored pencils (red, yellow, and green)

Directions: Distribute paper and pencils to participants. Invite them to reflect on their life journeys—personal and professional—thus far. Where have they been stopped in their work? Where have things gone well? Where have they yielded? Where have they changed directions—by choice, because of a detour, or for some other reason? Invite them to think about events and experiences that have been especially important to the direction their personal and professional lives have taken.

Next, ask them to draw road maps of their journey using traffic signals and road signs (red for stops, yellow for taking things slowly, green for going ahead) and marking yields, speed limits, caution signs (child at play, deer crossing, etc.), and U-turns. Suggest that they take 5 minutes to think quietly, perhaps jotting notes, and then 15 minutes to draw, making sure they capture both big and small moments that have had an impact on who and where they are today. When they are done, ask them to look at their work and ask themselves: What does the journey want to teach them? What do they notice about their lives? Is there a theme? Is there something they can see in the whole picture?

When you have finished this part of the activity, invite everyone to find a partner. One person will spend 5 minutes sharing whatever he chooses from his life drawing as the other person listens carefully and deeply. The listener's job is to practice being fully present to the speaker. Listeners should think of themselves as tape recorders: they can repeat what the other person says in words or by body language, and they can ask clarifying questions. The goal is to listen to someone else's story, not to give advice or tell your own story in response. Simply give the gift of truly hearing another.

Switch roles and repeat the process.

Wrap-up: Keep the pairs together. Share this quote: "Everything that happens to you is your teacher. . . . The secret is to learn to sit at the feet of your own life and be taught by it." —Polly Berends

With this activity, each person is given the gift of truly being heard. No one tries to fix anything; rather, each partner "plays back" what the other says so that both can hear their own voices and listen to their own inner wisdom. The partners also "play back" body language (slumps, sighs, more rapid speech, etc.)—signs that may indicate something more that is going on during the conversation that the person may want to think about later.

While participants are still with their partners, invite them to think about and share thoughts on this question: As you move forward from what has been toward what you long for in the future, what might the next couple of road signs be?

Big Group Wrap-up:
- You stepped back to look at your lives to see if you identified an underlying theme or purpose. Perhaps what you saw could be identified as a "spark," that heartbeat that fulfills you. How do we feed the sparks and the purpose in our lives? What role does knowing our sense of purpose and knowing our own sparks play in our lives?
- How can we help our youth discover their inner sparks?

As you leave today, remember the themes you identified that reoccur in your life, the elements that sustain you, and the passions that are dear to you. Build on those things. Be open to making changes based on who you are and what you are uniquely designed to do.

Key Elements: Communication, Celebration, Vision, Creative Problem Solving

Asset Categories: Constructive Use of Time, Support, Social Competencies, Positive Identity, Positive Values

Insider's Tip: The creative nature of this activity lets participants focus energies and have something to do (doodle, draw) with their hands while letting their minds think about the questions in a more casual way, which sometimes helps create the space needed for inner wisdom to speak. The activity lets them center their thoughts.

The use of partners to hear stories and to mirror back words and body language also provides a reflection that isn't often accessible. When someone says, "You said this . . ." and you hear what you said, you can decide if that's really what you meant or not. Sometimes we have to speak out loud to discover what we truly believe and mean.

Activity contributed by Rick Jackson and Janice Virtue, Center for Courage and Renewal

SOCIAL SHUFFLE

Purpose: To recognize biases in the way people treat one another and to change behavior accordingly

Estimated Time: 15–20 minutes

Supplies: Deck of cards (if you have more than 52 people, you will need an additional deck of cards)

Directions: Shuffle the cards, and give each person one card. Ask participants not to look at their cards, but rather to hold them out in front of them where others can see them, but they cannot.

Tell the group to mingle and engage in conversation—especially seeking people whom they believe have a higher-value card than their own or are holding the same suit. Each person should select a partner who is a "great find."

After several minutes, ask the group to "freeze" where they are to talk through the wrap-up questions with their partners (without peeking at their cards yet):

Wrap-up:
- Where do you fit in the deck? Are you a low card? A high card?
- What makes you think this?
- What did you see/hear/feel during this activity?
- How does this game mirror our actions in real life? How does our way of valuing play out in our workplace?
- Who are the low cards in your group? The high cards? The jokers?
- How did avoidance, tolerance, and/or appreciation affect this activity?
- Look at your card. What can you learn from this activity?

Key Elements: Communication, Working Together, Community Building

Asset Categories: Support, Social Competencies, Boundaries and Expectations, Positive Values

Activity contributed by Marilyn Peplau, New Richmond, Wisconsin

THE GREAT ESCAPE

Purpose: This activity explores the dilemma of competition versus cooperation

Estimated Time: 20 minutes

Supplies: 60 items representing gold coins

Directions: Explain the scenario: "You have been captured and are being held captive. As captives, you have been forced into a game of life-changing consequences where your strategy and good fortune can save your lives by securing enough money for your release. You will be divided into two teams, and you will play multiple rounds. You will have the choice to compete or cooperate in each round. The ultimate goal is to get out of captivity and get home. To do that, your team must gather a total of 30 coins to purchase your release."

This is the structure of the contest:
1. Give teams two minutes to decide on their strategy for gathering the needed money.
2. For each round, each team sends one representative to where you are standing, where they both put their hands behind their backs.
3. On the count of three, both representatives must present their choice between cooperating or competing by using a hand signal of holding up one finger (cooperate) or two fingers (compete).
4. Following every turn, reward each representative with a certain number of gold coins resulting from his choice (see below).
5. After the coins are distributed, congratulate the players. The players return to their teams for 30 seconds to strategize their next move.
6. Continue play until a team earns enough coins to secure their release.

Winning the coins:
    a. If both players decide to cooperate, give each one 3 gold coins.
    b. If one player decides to cooperate and the other opts to compete, then give the competitor 5 gold coins and the cooperator nothing.
    c. If both parties decide to compete and try to outdo each other, then give each one a single gold coin.

Example: If both players hold up 1 finger, representing cooperation, then give each team 3 coins. Congratulate them and send them back to their teams. Instruct them to strategize again (30 seconds) and then call up new representatives for the next round.

Note: If you have more than 20 minutes to dedicate to this activity, you can choose to have teams compete for a greater number of coins, or if you have less than 20 minutes, you can have them compete for a smaller number of coins. Just make sure to have them compete for a number of coins that is divisible by six, and have twice that many coins on hand.

Wrap-up: This game forces a decision in every round: *My actions represent my team. I have to make a choice each time: Am I about the good of my team or the good of everyone overall? Am I looking out only for myself or for my team as well?*

We make decisions to compete or cooperate every day. *Do I use information against a person or for her benefit? Do I want to see her fall so that I look better, or help her succeed so that we as a team are successful?* If we care about other people and the success of the team, we make it easier for others.

Ask the group:
- What was your intention in each round? How did you determine your team strategy?
- Apply the tactics of the game to life: How do you decide when to compete and when to cooperate? What goes into your daily decisions?
- How do you respond if and when you are wronged?
- How can we focus on cooperating for the overall good of our team, instead of competing?
- What are some of the areas in your life where you have to decide whether you'll compete or cooperate? How do you decide what you'll do?
- How does cooperation enhance community work and collaborations?
- How does competition negatively affect our asset-building efforts with young people?

Key Elements: Communication, Working Together, Team Building, Conflict Resolution

Asset Categories: Constructive Use of Time, Social Competencies, Boundaries and Expectations

Activity contributed by Bill Van de Griek, Nashville, Tennessee

TINY TEACH

Purpose: To help participants realize the importance of recognizing and respecting one another's gifts and talents

Estimated Time: 10–15 minutes

Supplies: None

Directions: Divide the group into pairs. Set up the activity by noting that all participants are resources and everyone has something to share with others. Give pairs 5 minutes to teach or tell each other about something they know well. For example, a person might share a secret apple pie recipe or a tap dance move, or teach a song in Chinese. Let players know you'll be asking for volunteers to share with the group what they learned. Allow additional time if players need it. Let as many groups volunteer to demonstrate or describe their new knowledge as time allows.

Wrap-up:
- What did this activity help you realize about your own abilities or those of your teammates?
- Why is it important to keep "digging deeper" to get to know and respect your colleagues?
- How does it affect your work culture when you take time to recognize and respect one another's gifts and talents?

Key Elements: Communication, Working Together, Community Building, Celebration

Asset Categories: Empowerment, Commitment to Learning, Social Competencies, Constructive Use of Time

Insider's Tip: Consider using this game in tandem with Each One Teach One on page below.

Adapted from Great Group Games *by Susan Ragsdale and Ann Saylor*

EACH ONE TEACH ONE

Purpose: To help participants understand and learn about diverse priorities and strategies in youth work

Estimated Time: 12–15 minutes

Supplies: None

Directions: Ask participants to think of one quality that is important for young people to grasp, then get into pairs and share the qualities they thought of, plus one strategy to help youth begin to experience that quality. For example, one strategy for building the attribute of friendship is to show genuine interest in another person and ask questions to encourage getting to know each other. Allow 4 minutes, during which people will have 2 minutes to share and 2 minutes to learn from their partners. Ask volunteers to share the strategies they learned from one another.

Wrap-up: Each one of us has the ability to teach someone else about healthy youth development factors and strategies. Just think of how positive and effective it would be if each of us took time to share our knowledge and ideas with one another and with other adults who have an impact on young people.

Key Elements: Communication, Team Building, Vision, Celebration, Community Building

Asset Categories: Empowerment, Support, Constructive Use of Time, Commitment to Learning, Social Competencies, Positive Identity

Insider's Tip: This can also be used as part of an ongoing process of sharing current research, tips, and findings within your group. Allow participants 5–10 minutes to review the literature or notes from a training, and then let them share key findings with others.

MISSION TO MARS

Purpose: To practice problem-solving skills and to use the exercise as a springboard for discussing group gifts and dynamics

Estimated Time: 10–12 minutes

Supplies: For each team, one set of 10–12 interlocking blocks (such as Legos) that are identical in size and shape (color is irrelevant) and one plastic bag; a box or a towel

Preparation: Use interlocking blocks to build an object that looks like it could be part of a spaceship and then hide it under a box or a towel. For each team, put 10–12 identical block pieces into a plastic bag.

Directions: Divide the group into teams of four or five. Give participants the following scenario or create your own:

> Secret agents of a distant country have stolen a vital part for a top-secret space launcher. If they learn how the part works, they will ruin our plan to be the first to land on the planet Mars. Your mission is to go into the secret lab of the enemy, study the part for one minute, and memorize what you see. We can sneak you in, but the secret police will search you as you leave—therefore, you cannot touch the part or take it with you. You must memorize how it is put together and then re-create it from memory.

Uncover the part you built and allow the teams to look at it for 1 minute. Then cover it again. Give the teams their bags of blocks and ask them to build the part from memory. The shape must be the same; color is not important in this mission.

Compare the teams' work to the original to see how they did.

Wrap-up:
- Talk about the process. What happened in each team?
- How well did the team work together? How well did the team communicate?
- What gifts emerged from each of the teammates? For example, who was the encourager? Who showed a gift for memorization? Who was good at putting together the object, or at keeping people focused? What about making sure everyone was heard and respected? Did anyone emerge as a leader?

This game brings out the different gifts we all have. It shows how we're uniquely wired. It can also show where we don't have particular gifts and illustrate that, as a team, we have to learn to lean on the strengths each person brings in order to maximize team efforts.

When we work together as a team and understand our roles, how we contribute to the mission, and how valuable that is, then almost any mission is very possible.

Key Elements: Communication, Working Together, Team Building, Creative Problem Solving, Conflict Resolution

Asset Categories: Empowerment, Support, Boundaries and Expectations, Constructive Use of Time, Social Competencies, Commitment to Learning

Activity contributed by Jim Williams, Junction City, Kansas

ANIMAL CORNERS

Purpose: To help participants think about building and maintaining strong relationships

Estimated Time: 5–7 minutes

Supplies: None

Directions: Ask participants to move to the corner of the room that best represents how they would finish this statement:

"To build and maintain strong relationships with colleagues, I think it is most helpful to act like a German shepherd, a border collie, a greyhound, or a Chihuahua." Point to a different corner of the room for each of the animals. Ask each person to quickly walk to the corner that represents her response to the sentence shared. Repeat if needed.

After participants move to their corners, ask them to mingle for a few minutes within their corners, introducing themselves and sharing why they selected that animal. Ask for a volunteer in each corner to tell the large group why they chose that animal.

Share the next sentence: "To build and maintain supportive relationships with young people, I think it is most helpful to act like an ostrich, a goose, a wolf, or a lion." Point to each corner as you call out one of the animal groups. Let people move, and repeat the previous sharing process.

Wrap-up:
- What are some reasons these animals would help build and maintain strong relationships with colleagues and/or young people?
- Is there a difference between the way you view building relationships with colleagues and with young people?

Listening to all the descriptors of building and maintaining strong relationships, ponder one way you are especially strong in relationship building. Share that aspect with a neighbor.

With that same neighbor, take a moment to consider one way you need to sharpen your relationship-building skills. Commit within your group to building strong and healthy relationships—with colleagues, young people, and other people you spend time with.

Key Elements: Communication, Vision, Team Building, Community Building, Celebration

Asset Categories: Support, Boundaries and Expectations, Social Competencies, Positive Identity

GUM BALL COUNT

Purpose: To illustrate the influence of groups on individuals and of individuals on groups

Estimated Time: 20 minutes

Supplies: Jar of gum balls (or Froot Loops, Skittles, or candy corn); paper and pen for each person

Directions: Give everyone a piece of paper and something to write with.

Hold up a jar filled with gum balls, and tell participants to silently guess how many are in the jar. They are not to discuss their guesses with anyone. Have them write down their guesses on paper and label them #1.

Now ask participants to pair up, share their guesses, debate the number, and together determine a new best guess, which they will record on their individual sheets as guess #2.

Have pairs form groups of four to reassess their guesses, agree on a number, and record their guesses as #3 on their papers. Repeat the process as often as desired. Just be sure to go back to a final individual round in which each person makes a last independent guess using the information that they gained during the discussions. Ask people to share their guesses, and then reveal the actual number of candies in the jar. Ask participants to circle on their papers the guess that was closest to the correct number.

Note: With a small group, you can list a person's first guess on a sheet of paper in the front of the room and then that person's last guess. Go around the entire group to get everyone's answers.

Wrap-up: Discuss the process and how it influenced each person's final decision.
- How many people were closest when they guessed by themselves?
- Did you make a change between your first and last individual guesses? Which was closer?
- How were your decisions influenced by other people? Was it for the better? Or not?
- In life, do other people influence you? Is their influence for the better or not?
- Are you influenced by the young people you know? By adults? How?
- How can we influence others in positive ways and build on their strengths?

Alternate Wrap-up: The process of research is similar to what we just did. A researcher looks at an issue such as positive youth development—just as we looked at a jar full of gum balls—forms a theory, then compares notes and discusses the theory with other researchers, and eventually formulates a revised theory.

With positive youth development, we know that youth at their best need 31 to 40 of the Developmental Assets in their lives. Young people experience an average of 20.1 assets, which is far too few. However, if we work together and are positive influences on the youth around us and help them discover their own "gum ball goodness," we can help them increase the number of assets in their lives.

Key Element Categories: Communication, Working Together, Vision, Community Building, Conflict Resolution, Creative Problem Solving

Asset Categories: Empowerment, Support, Boundaries and Expectations, Positive Identity

THIS IS A WHAT?

Purpose: To simulate a busy work environment with multiple tasks and confused messaging, then to talk about strategies for clear communication and staying focused amidst chaos and confusion

Estimated Time: 10 minutes

Supplies: Two objects that can be passed from hand to hand around a circle, such as a ball, cap, shoe, hacky sack, etc. (We recommend two goofy-looking stuffed animals that fit the names used in the directions.)

Directions: The group sits in a circle. As the leader, you start by holding one of the objects in your hand (let's say it's a yellow stuffed animal). Look at the person sitting to your right, Amy, and say, "This is a yellow-bellied sapsucker." She responds, "A what?" You say, "A yellow-bellied sapsucker." She takes the animal and says, "Oh, a yellow-bellied sapsucker."

Amy then turns to the next person, Joe, and starts the same interaction with him, except that when Joe asks her, "A what?" she turns back to you and asks, "A what?" You restate, "A yellow-bellied sapsucker," then Amy turns and repeats it to Joe, who says, "Oh, a yellow-bellied sapsucker." And so it continues—a big game of "Pete and Repeat" all the way around the circle. Each new person to receive the animal will ask the previous person in the circle "A what?" who will ask the previous person "A what?" and so on, until it gets back to you to tell them "A yellow-bellied sapsucker."

Meanwhile, start a second item going around the circle in the *opposite* direction (let's say it's a green stuffed animal). Turn to the person to your left, Greg, and say, "This is a spineyback-horned toad." Greg asks, "A what?" Repeat, "A spineyback-horned toad." Greg says, "Oh, a spineyback-horned toad." Thus the passing and "Pete and Repeat" of conversation goes around the other way.

Chaos erupts when the two items meet at the same point and the poor person in the middle tries to keep the two conversations going and intact. The conversation train generally will get all muddled. Laughter ensues and sometimes tears flow!

Wrap-up:
- Did this game feel more like chaos or calm?
- How did you respond to this task? Did you get really focused, or did you just kick back and enjoy the chaos?
- How did it feel to juggle multiple items and communication streams?
- Did your messages ever get confused or off track?
- Apply the connection to your work world. How is this game a picture of what can happen at work?
- When faced with chaos, how do you respond?
- How do you handle juggling multiple projects and mixed messages? How do you keep things straight and headed in the right direction?
- What are specific strategies we can follow in our group to limit or deal with the chaos and confusion?
- How can we best create clarity amidst the chaos and confusion?

Key Elements: Communication, Working Together, Teamwork

Asset Categories: Support, Social Competencies, Boundaries and Expectations, Positive Values, Empowerment

Insider's Tip: This activity works well to use before the Team Continuum Dialogue on page 59.

Activity contributed by Bill Van de Griek, Nashville, Tennessee

TRUST

NEVER JUDGE A BOOK BY ITS COVER

Purpose: To illustrate how assumptions can get in the way of understanding and good communication

Estimated Time: 15–20 minutes

Supplies: Chart paper, marker; paper and a pen for each team

Preparation: List on chart paper these categories: age (be kind), race, marital status, place of birth (city, state), hobbies, parents' occupations, religion, first job, favorite movie genre, current occupation, what I thought I would do for a career, type of car I drive, educational degree(s).

Directions: Divide the group into table teams of six to eight. Invite table group members to confer and guess the information about you, the facilitator, and to record their guesses on paper. (**Note:** If you are working with a group that knows you well, identify someone else ahead of time to be the subject, someone who is comfortable sharing information from the categories list.)

Give the groups 5 minutes or less to confer and determine their answers. When time is up, go around the room, one table at a time, and ask each group to share its answer to the first question. Give the correct information and comment as desired. Repeat the process for each category.

Wrap-up: This activity shows how easy it is to make a judgment call or guess traits, values, and characteristics about another person—and how often those guesses are actually inaccurate. We make assumptions based on what we see. Judging a book by its cover is a human tendency that often proves to be wrong. Our assumptions come from many things: how we grew up, our own view of how things should be, our past experiences, family, background, and culture. This tendency to "prejudge" gets in the way of reaching out to know others; it creates barriers to communication and understanding.

- Do you do anything that gets in the way of people knowing the real you?
- In what ways do you have a habit of judging people before you really know them? How does that affect your relationships with them?
- How can we overcome the barriers and assumptions that could block understanding? Invite the group to come up with strategies for overcoming bias.
- Where else does this activity apply in our work and lives?

Key Elements: Communication, Conflict Resolution, Working Together, Community Building

Asset Categories: Social Competencies, Support, Positive Identity

DIVERSITY BUTTONS

Purpose: To illustrate our natural tendency to prejudge others and to identify ways to overcome that tendency

Estimated Time: 20–35 minutes

Supplies: Box of random buttons or keys, flip chart and chart paper, marker

Preparation: Draw a vertical line in the center of the flip chart to divide the chart into two columns

Directions: Divide the group into teams of three to four participants. Give each team a handful of buttons and ask them to think about how they would separate their buttons. What attributes might they choose as a basis for separating them? For example, they might separate their buttons by color.

Have the groups separate their buttons by one attribute. After 30 seconds, ask groups to report how they separated their buttons. Chart the answers in the left-hand column; leave the right column blank for now.

Ask participants to identify another way to separate their buttons that is *not* already listed on the chart. Continue going around the room, asking groups to share answers three or four more times and recording all answers in the left column of the flip chart. (Trainer's note: Take whatever participants give you. Don't question the ways they think to separate the buttons.)

Once the list is complete, make the following statement: "We form prejudices about things we're not familiar with. When we see a person, we prejudge that individual before getting to know her or him."

Go down the list and solicit comments on the various button attributes the groups came up with, seeing how they might also describe differences in human beings. State the attributes in the form of a question. For example, "What might *shape* mean when we identify that with human beings? What might *old vs. new* mean when it comes to applying that characteristic to humans?" Record the groups' answers in the right-hand column next to each attribute. Note that there are no "correct" answers, because we all perceive things differently.

Discuss: Let participants respond to each of the following questions. (Make the italicized key points if they are not mentioned by anyone in the group.)

- Now, what's the purpose of buttons? *(To* connect *both sides of a piece of clothing. All buttons connect two things. Yes, they might be decorative, but they are used to connect two things together.)*
- What do we as human beings need? *(To connect with other humans.)*
- What do we let stand in the way of connecting with each other? *(All those attributes from which we "prejudge" another.)*
- How do we get beyond the things that stand in the way?
- Knowing that we may encounter any of these "types" of colleagues, youth, or parents, how do we get beyond prejudging other people to truly respect who they are, to build authentic relationships, and to grow together?

For 10 minutes, have button teams work to create a "top five" list of how to move beyond the distractions of the attributes to truly appreciating the *humans* who have those attributes.

Ask groups to share their ideas.

Wrap-up: Invite participants to determine the key idea(s) that they want to remember to help them avoid prejudging others.

Key Elements: Interaction, Fun, Working Together, Communication, Community Building

Asset Categories: Support, Empowerment, Positive Identity, Social Competencies, Commitment to Learning

Activity contributed by Ruth Cox, Nashville, Tennessee

COMMUNITY PUZZLE

Purpose: To help participants think imaginatively about the power of groups and communities to accomplish a common vision

Estimated Time: 12–15 minutes

Supplies: A complete 36–60-piece jigsaw puzzle; three or four resealable plastic sandwich bags

Preparation: Assemble the puzzle ahead of time. Carefully take the puzzle apart in three or four sections, with approximately 12–20 pieces in each section. Put each section in a separate plastic sandwich bag, pieces not connected.

Directions: Divide the large group into three or four small groups. Give each small group a bag of puzzle pieces and ask them to distribute the pieces to their team members. Challenge the group to assemble the puzzle in 5 minutes or less.

Facilitator's Note: Do not tell the groups that the pieces belong to one large puzzle, and do not show them the picture they are working toward. As they start to piece the puzzle together, they will realize that they need to merge the pieces with the other groups' pieces.

Wrap-up:
- How many teams were there in this game?
- Too often people and organizations operate in isolated silos, without ever realizing that all the players (individuals, departments, employees, supervisors, board members, etc.) are actually on the same team.
- If you had operated as three or four divided teams for the duration of the activity, what level of success would you have achieved?
- What made you successful? What were the keys to success?
- Success requires give and take in regard to responsibilities, leadership, cooperation, credit, and recognition. It requires seeing a bigger picture, teamwork, and connecting pieces for a common vision.

- How is teamwork like a jigsaw puzzle?

Variation: Remove some of the pieces of the puzzle so that it cannot be completed. Talk about the gaps that occur when all the players aren't engaged in working toward the same vision, or when youth don't have all the assets they need.

Wrap-up:
- What pieces are needed to make our vision for youth work come together?
- What pieces make up a whole life for youth? What pieces do they need in their lives to be complete?
- Which pieces can we put into place for them?

Key Elements: Communication, Working Together, Community Building, Vision, Creative Problem Solving

Asset Categories: Support, Social Competencies, Boundaries and Expectations, Positive Values

MIXED MESSAGES

Purpose: To illustrate the importance of integrity, clarity, and honesty in our interactions with each other and in communicating with youth

Estimated Time: 8–12 minutes

Supplies: A small object to give away, such as a container of Tic Tacs or a mug

Directions: Ask a volunteer to leave the room. While the volunteer is out, divide the rest of the group into two teams. Tell them that you are going to play the game "Hot and Cold," and the volunteer is going to try to find an object. Instruct one team to guide the volunteer *toward* the object. Ask the other team to guide the volunteer *away* from the object and toward another item in the room, such as a pen or a notebook that is in the opposite direction from the object. Tell the groups that they will do this *at the same time.*

Call the volunteer back in. Tell him that the group will guide him to an object by saying "hot" or "cold." Begin play.

After a minute or two, ask the volunteer: "How do you feel about this game? What do you think about your chances for succeeding?"

Discuss:
- How did it feel to be on the team misguiding the volunteer?
- How did it feel to be on the team guiding the volunteer honestly?
- At its core, this game had inconsistent messages. How do inconsistent or mixed messages hurt a team?
- Think about our work with youth. How do mixed messages affect young people?
- What are some of the mixed messages that youth get? Where do those messages come from?

- What is the core message we hope to communicate to the youth we work with?
- How can we uphold our own integrity and consistency in the face of the many mixed messages youth get every day?
- What ideas do you have for sharing consistent positive messages with youth in the community?

After a brief discussion, award the giveaway object to the volunteer for being a good sport.

Wrap-up: This game is about us as a team and us as role models for youth. It's important for us to remain as clear and honest as we possibly can with each other and with youth. We should ask questions if we're confused or don't understand something. We should strive for clear communication, understanding, and honesty in our interactions with each other.

What will you remember about this exercise tomorrow?

Key Elements: Communication, Working Together, Community Building

Asset Categories: Empowerment, Social Competencies, Positive Values

Adapted from an activity by Bob Wittman, from the booklet Taking Asset Building Personally: A Guide for Planning and Facilitating Study Groups *(Minneapolis: Search Institute, 1999)*

SHIFTING GEARS

Purpose: To help participants reflect on the progress an organization or community can make in regard to positive youth development

Estimated Time: 10 minutes

Supplies: Shifting Gears handout and a writing utensil for each person

Directions: Invite participants to think individually about the shifts listed in the handout and determine which shift is the easiest for each of them to make and which is the most difficult. Then ask them to form pairs to talk about the shifts and identify the easiest and toughest ones. Have the pairs brainstorm ways to make the hardest shift easier.

Wrap-up: Our work is about transformation. We want to transform our communities and the experiences our youth have. Transformation, however, begins with ourselves—our attitudes, our thoughts and perspectives, how we think and act. A positive youth development perspective calls for us to look at things from a strength-based approach rather than from a deficit-based approach. The attitudes in this activity reflect some of the transformation work we need to do within ourselves and within the community.

- What steps are you personally taking toward becoming the best you can be for young people?

Shifting Gears

FROM:		TO:
Problem focus	⟶	**Positive focus**
Youth as problems	⟶	**Youth as resources**
Reactive behavior	⟶	**Proactive behavior**
Blaming	⟶	**Claiming responsibility**
Professionals' role	⟶	**Everyone's job**
Crisis management	⟶	**Vision building**
Competition	⟶	**Cooperation**
Despair	⟶	**Hope**

- What steps can we take as a group to shift gears and focus more fully on drawing out the strengths and potential of the youth you interact with?
- What gets in the way of making progress toward the shifts?
- What can we do to keep moving toward progress?

Key Elements: Communication, Community Building, Creative Problem Solving, Vision

Asset Categories: Support, Empowerment, Positive Identity, Commitment to Learning, Positive Values, Boundaries and Expectations

FROM TROUBLES TO TREASURES

Purpose: To help participants assist each other in meeting the challenges they face in their work

Estimated Time: 14–20 minutes

Supplies: One blank (or recycled) sheet of paper and a writing utensil for each person, a large empty basket or box, tape

Directions: Ask participants to take a moment to think about challenges they are facing in their work with young people and briefly write about one at the top of a blank sheet of paper, being sure to include any details necessary for a consultant team to understand the issue.

Invite participants to wad their "troubles" (papers) into a ball and toss them into the basket or box.

At some point during your meeting, ask participants to get into teams of three.

Toss each team one paper ball from the basket. Tell the teams to flatten the papers, read about the challenges, and then spend 3–5 minutes brainstorming possible ways to meet/overcome the challenges and write their ideas directly on the sheets.

Tape up completed sheets in a central place where people can look at them during breaks or afterward.

Repeat this activity twice more during the meeting so that all sheets from the basket are discussed. At the end of the meeting, invite individuals to take their original sheets with them.

Variation: Form teams of four to eight people. Ask each team to write down one challenge they would like input on from others in the room and describe the challenge in detail so that others have a clear understanding of the issues involved. The team then passes its sheet to another team. (Establish a rotation.) The second team spends around 5 minutes brainstorming potential solutions. Repeat the rotation until all teams have seen each sheet or until your time is up. The original team reviews potential solutions and identifies what they would like to implement.

Key Elements: Communication, Working Together, Community Building, Creative Problem Solving, Conflict Resolution

Asset Categories: Empowerment, Constructive Use of Time, Support, Commitment to Learning, Positive Identity

Insider's Tip: This is a great activity to intersperse throughout a meeting, or it can be done at one set-aside time.

TRANSFORMATION STATIONS

Purpose: To help participants identify attitudes that help—as well as hinder—teamwork

Estimated Time: 10–15 minutes

Supplies: None

Directions: Describe the process of a continuum dialogue to the group: You will read two opposite statements, and participants will place themselves somewhere on an imaginary arc between the two opposing statements. Designate one end of the arc for the first statement and the other end for the second statement. Read aloud one set of statements, and allow everyone to choose where to stand on the arc.

Once everyone has made a choice of where to stand, ask for volunteers to explain why they chose their positions. As with any group activity, participants should show respect, give full attention to the people who are talking, and not challenge or tease them. And, as people listen to and reflect on what's been said, they can change their minds and move to different positions. If they want to say why they moved, give them an opportunity to do so. Encourage participants to be honest and to consider what they are most likely to do on a daily basis rather than what they *think* they should do. After they have finished explaining their positions, read aloud another set of statements and again allow participants to find their places on the arc. Repeat as often as you wish.

Choose from the following options the continuum dialogue statements that best reflect issues your group needs to explore.

(a) I am guarded about what I share in teams.　　(b) I freely express my feelings and ideas in teams.

(a) I feel there is one right way to go.　　(b) I feel there are multiple paths to achieve our goal.

(a) I hold other team members accountable for their actions toward others.　　(b) How other team members behave around people different from me doesn't really concern me.

(a) I focus on the problem (crisis management).　　(b) I focus on the solution (vision-oriented).

(a) I tend to see reality.	(b) I tend to see possibility.
(a) I tend to focus on the value of each team member and what each has to contribute.	(b) I tend to focus on just a few people's gifts and contributions.
(a) I tend to be more reactive in situations.	(b) I tend to be more proactive in situations.
(a) There is only one leader.	(b) Everyone can lead.

Wrap-up: We are often looking for ideas and ways to work with youth to transform our communities. To have the best impact on others, we must first find ways to transform ourselves. Working with others as a cohesive unit often requires a shift in the way we think and act, or a different way of looking at things. The attitudes we addressed in this activity reflect the potential for attitudes that can help or hinder teamwork.

- What gave you food for thought from this activity?
- Which attitudes are helpful in cohesive teams?
- Were there any attitudes that you might want to work on or improve for the sake of the group?
- What potential application do you see from what we've talked about?

Key Elements: Communication, Working Together, Team Building, Community Building, Conflict Resolution

Asset Categories: Support, Empowerment, Positive Values, Positive Identity, Social Competencies

CARS

Purpose: To emphasize the need for trust and personal responsibility among participants

Estimated Time: 10–15 minutes

Supplies: None

Directions: Ask participants to form pairs, one person standing directly behind the other. If the group is too large or if you have an odd number, you can ask people to stand to the side and wait for instructions on their role in the game.

Tell the participants that they will be playing the "Cars" game. The object of the game is to move around the room without crashing into anything, including other cars. The people in front are "cars" and the people behind them are "drivers." Ask the drivers to put their hands on the shoulders of the cars to steer them. The catch is that the cars have to keep their eyes closed while they are being driven; they have to rely on their drivers to keep them from crashing into anything.

Ask the cars to place their elbows at their sides and their hands out in front of them to serve as "bumpers." Invite any additional participants to be stop signs, speed bumps, or something else in or near the road; two people might join their hands above their heads to form a tunnel.

Ask for any clarifications, and then tell participants to start their engines and begin to move around the room. After a few minutes, ask pairs to switch places and let the cars become the drivers. Give everyone a chance to participate.

Wrap-up:

- How did it feel to be a car in this activity? Did you feel nervous about letting someone else guide you around the room with your eyes closed?
- What was it like to be a driver? Did you feel like you had to be especially cautious?
- How does this activity reflect our lives and our experiences in community building or working together as a team?
- Sometimes it can be difficult to share with others what is precious to us. We wonder, "Will others care as much as I do?" and "Will they work to protect it?" This is what trust and responsibility are all about. We have to be willing to let others share our trials as well as our triumphs.
- Take it one step deeper: What are the things we care deeply about with regard to young people? What strengths do we hope they have? What do we hope to protect within them?

Key Elements: Communication, Working Together, Creative Problem Solving

Asset Categories: Boundaries and Expectations, Support, Positive Values, Social Competencies, Positive Identity

Activity contributed by Jim Williams, Junction City, Kansas

OBSTACLE WALK

Purpose: To help participants identify attitudes that hinder as well as help their work

Estimated Time: 15–25 minutes

Supplies: Chart paper, marker, tape, obstacles (use objects that are on hand in the space: chairs, tables, notebooks, paper)

Preparation: Create an obstacle course confined in a narrow area marked by tape on the floor.

Directions: Point out the pathway established in the room and inform the group that it leads to success, but there are obstacles along the way. The group must make its way along the path. The challenge is that the group must stay connected at all times, and they can't touch any of the obstacles or step outside the boundaries marked by tape.

Before the group begins to work toward success, ask them to identify obstacles that get in the way of positive youth development (or obstacles to teamwork, or to having an impact on youth, or whatever issue you wish to address).

Chart their answers. Challenge the group to narrow down the list to the four or five most challenging obstacles for the team to overcome. Star those obstacles. Ask for a couple of volunteers to find four or five additional objects from the room to represent the starred obstacles. The objects they select should symbolize the perceived strength and size of the obstacles they are to represent. Have the volunteers place the objects in the pathway.

Instruct the group to join up at one end of the pathway. Remind them that they must stick to the pathway that leads to success and not step over boundaries or step on obstacles, and they must stay connected in some way (by holding hands, linking arms, placing their hands on another person's shoulders, etc.). If at any time someone steps over a boundary, touches an obstacle, or loses contact with the others, the whole group must start over. Let the group work its way through the maze.

If desired, add levels of challenge: select some participants to be unable to see, walk, and/or speak. Accordingly, those who are blind must keep their eyes closed, those who are unable to walk must crawl or be carried, and those who are mute are not allowed to speak.

Wrap-up:
- How well did you do on your road to success?
- What challenges did you face?
- How did you respond to the challenges of the maze? How did you work through them?
- How is this activity an illustration of our work?
- In the starting conversation, you named obstacles you face. How do you work through those obstacles? How do you overcome them?
- What obstacles do *you* put in the way to success? How often do *you* put up obstacles to success?
- One of the tasks and goals of achieving success was to stay connected. Why was that an established expectation?
- Why is staying connected important? Why is it a key element of youth work?

Key Elements: Communication, Working Together, Teamwork, Vision, Creative Problem Solving, Conflict Resolution

Asset Categories: Support, Social Competencies, Empowerment, Boundaries and Expectations

ELECTRIC CURRENT

Purpose: To illustrate the need for and importance of trust (in ourselves and in each other) within teams

Estimated Time: 15–20 minutes

Supplies: Ball, Frisbee, or some other object to pick up (one per team); a quarter

Directions: Divide the group into two teams of 5 to 30 participants. Ask each team to sit in a line, holding hands; place the team's ball behind the last player in the line. Give instructions for the game: Each team is going to generate electric currents. The goal is to be the first team to create nine volts (that is, reach nine points). Teams collect volts when they successfully pass a current through their line.

To pass a current and collect a volt, your team must successfully read the "volt meter" signal, which will be given to the first person in each line, and pass the current down the line to the last person, who will then pick up the ball and bring it to the front of the line. The first team to bring the ball to the front of their line collects a volt.

Here are the rules of engagement: All participants except the first person in each line must have their eyes closed during play. The first person in each line cannot talk.

Play begins when you flip a coin. Make sure that team leaders can see the result of the coin flip. If it lands on heads, team leaders rush to send their current down the line so their team can be the first to pick up the ball. Squeezing the hand of the next person in line sends the current down the line to the last person, who picks up the ball and runs it to the front. The first team to send the current all the way down, get the ball, and bring it to the front collects a volt.

However, if the coin lands on tails and the current is sent through the team and the ball is picked up, then the team loses a point. Teams also lose points if eyes are open, or if the first person in the line talks.

Remind groups before each flip to close their eyes. If desired, you can say "flip" before you flip the coin to signal them to be ready.

Play until one of the teams collects nine volts. Rotate the first-player position by asking the two last persons in line to stay up front when they bring the ball.

Wrap-up:
- What happened in this game? What worked? What didn't?
- How might this activity serve as a picture of our work together in the community?
- Trust played a role. You had to trust each person to do his job. You had to trust that you would be given what was needed when it was needed. The task called for trust in leadership.
- This activity could also highlight the juggling we have to do: meeting goals, making the "current" (i.e., the impact) we want to make in the community and with youth, working with each other, being responsible for our own part of the work, and at the same time supporting each other under stress!
- How *do* we support each other under stress?

- How did we do in the game when mistakes were made? How do we do in the real world when deadlines are missed or instructions are misunderstood?
- How do we support each other to keep working toward our goal?

Key Elements: Communication, Working Together, Creative Problem Solving, Work-Life Balance

Asset Categories: Support, Empowerment, Social Competencies, Boundaries and Expectations

Developed in the field by educators affiliated with the National School Reform Faculty Adapted with permission from www.nsrfharmony.org

MUMBLE JUMBLE

Purpose: To reinforce the importance of responsibility and effort in future teamwork

Estimated Time: 10 minutes

Supplies: Two or more jumbo children's puzzles with 6–10 pieces each (enough for every participant to have 1 puzzle piece)

Preparation: Shuffle the puzzle pieces, so that pieces from multiple puzzles are intermixed

Directions: Give each participant one random puzzle piece. (If there are puzzle pieces left over, place them in a centralized location where participants will assemble the puzzle.) Participants keep their puzzle pieces to themselves until the leader says "Go!" At this point, participants try to quickly locate the other members of the group with the pieces they need to form pictures. Encourage groups to celebrate when they complete their pictures.

Wrap-up:
- How important was your individual piece to the process of working the puzzle?
- Can you successfully work a puzzle without all of the pieces?
- How might the puzzle be symbolic of the way we work together as a group?
- How important is it that each of us gives full effort to our responsibilities within the group?

Key Elements: Communication, Creative Problem Solving, Working Together, Conflict Resolution

Asset Categories: Support, Constructive Use of Time, Boundaries and Expectations, Positive Values, Positive Identity

Insider's Tip: This is a good activity for breaking a large group into smaller groups.

Activity contributed by Flora Sanchez, Albuquerque, New Mexico

BOXES OF RISK

Purpose: To help participants ponder how levels of comfort, risk, and danger affect personal growth

Estimated Time: 20 minutes

Supplies: Masking tape

Preparation: Use masking tape to outline three concentric squares on the floor. The largest square should have room for the entire group to stand comfortably within it; then create two squares within the large square, each one smaller than the first. The smallest box should be just large enough for the whole group if they stand very closely together.

Directions: Show the group the three concentric squares and say, "These boxes represent three emotional states. The outer box represents comfort, the middle box represents a feeling of risk, and the inner box is where you feel a sense of danger. I will be reading a series of statements and scenarios. After each statement, I want you to step into the box where that statement puts you personally: comfort, risk, or danger." Remind the group that this is a high-risk activity that requires a high level of trust. There are no incorrect answers—each response is a personal response. Confidentiality is key, so remember that what is said (verbally or nonverbally) in the group should stay within the group.

Start by reading a scenario, allowing participants to move within the boxes, and then asking one or two volunteers to explain how they chose that box to represent their response.

Statements and scenarios (adapt these to fit your group):
1. You are asked to climb to the top of an extension ladder (icebreaker example).
2. Your boss really likes the program that you've created and asks you to give a presentation to the board.
3. Someone comes to you distraught because she's pregnant unexpectedly, and she's turned to you for help.
4. You become aware that someone is in a dangerous home situation, but he hasn't yet told you. You are concerned for his safety.
5. You heard someone make a derogatory remark, and you thought it was inappropriate. You know you need to say something.
6. You are caught in the middle of a conflict between two close colleagues/friends.
7. Your boss has an idea for the group that you don't think will work, and you need to speak up and voice your disagreement.
8. You have a dream for a new project or business. The economy is bad. How comfortable are you in going after your dream?
9. You have news to give your friends and family that you know will shock them. How comfortable are you in being honest and sharing your news?
10. Someone is gossiping about another person in a hurtful way, and you know you need to tell her to stop.

Wrap-up:
- What were your first thoughts when you heard the areas: comfort, risk, and danger?
- What do these areas mean to you? How did they originally translate in your filters?
- What puts people in risk mode?
- How do we help people move out of their comfort zone, that place where it's easy to get lazy or apathetic?
- How do we move people out of danger and into the risk area?
  (Note: *Danger is where we are in defense and/or survival mode.*)
- What can we do to pull you out of comfort and put you in the risk mode for the sake of learning and growing?
- What are you willing to take risks for? Are there common factors that make it easier for you to take risks?

The key learning to take away from this activity is that the most effective learning happens when people are in risk, not in comfort or danger. For what will we take a risk today?

Key Elements: Conflict Resolution, Creative Problem Solving, Communication

Asset Categories: Support, Boundaries and Expectations, Empowerment, Social Competencies, Positive Identity

Activity created with Anderson Williams, Nashville, Tennessee

IMPACT

THE WISDOM OF YOUTH

Purpose: To get participants to think about the people and places that had an impact on them as young people

Estimated Time: 10 minutes

Supplies: Paper, pencils

Directions: Invite participants to write down some of the most powerful positive experiences they had when they were 12–16 years old (or whatever age range you want to put in), experiences that stand out as having had a significant impact on them. Give them 2–3 minutes to reflect and write.

Give them another couple of minutes to think about the impact they want to have on the youth they know.

Invite participants to find a partner and share stories.

Wrap-up: We recalled and celebrated powerful moments in our own childhoods. We shared the impact we want to have on youth. What will you remember about this activity? What resonates from this experience?

Key Elements: Communication, Vision, Celebration, Community Building

Asset Categories: Support, Empowerment, Positive Values, Social Competencies, Boundaries and Expectations, Positive Identity

Insider's Tip: This activity can be used to lead participants into a vision process. Its value is in helping participants connect more intentionally with the age group they are working with by recalling themselves at that age and then sharing their hopes for youth now.

It can also be used as an icebreaker question or as a warm-up activity before exploring strategies for positive youth development.

BOX IN, BOX OUT

Purpose: To get participants thinking about how valuable young people are as individuals and in our communities

Estimated Time: 5–10 minutes

Supplies: A box, paper, and writing utensils for each group

Directions: Divide your group into teams of four players. Tell the group that what they see before them really isn't a box. Ask the teams to take 2 minutes to think of as many possibilities of what the box *could* be as they can. Encourage them to draw rather than make a list.

When time is up, encourage participants to walk around and look at all the possibilities crafted by others. Once everyone is finished and seated, debrief.

Wrap-up: The power of this exercise is in recognizing possibilities, imagination, and thinking about the potential of what could be. You weren't limited by what you saw before you. You weren't confined to a box; rather, you thought outside the box.

- Which of the drawings within your own group did you like best? Which of the other group creations did you especially appreciate?
- What are your observations about how often or not people take others at face value? How often do you think people just see the box?
- In our work with young people, how often do others "see" them as "boxes" and have preconceived notions of what that means and who they are?
- How often is our attention drawn to possibilities and potential as opposed to packaging or limitations or usefulness?
- What would happen if we took time to look closely and creatively for potential and each person's unique strengths and gifts? How would it affect your work, if you made a habit of seeing the best potential in each of your young people? In each of your colleagues?
- What are some of the strategies you use to remember to look for the good in each person and to see that individual's potential?
- What are some of the strategies you use in your work to engage youth in opportunities that show others their value and use their strengths?

Key Elements: Vision, Creative Problem Solving, Community Building

Asset Categories: Support, Boundaries and Expectations, Empowerment, Positive Identity

MY STARPERSON

Purpose: To help participants think about their roles and impact; to help the group set goals for future work

Estimated Time: 10–12 minutes

Supplies: Starperson handouts, writing utensils, music

Directions: Give each person a starperson handout. Tell the group that you are going to ask a series of questions, and you want them to fill in their starpeople with words or phrases that answer the questions. Let them know that they will be sharing their work at the end of the activity, so they can filter their thoughts and words accordingly. Play quiet music and ask participants to write without talking.

Ask the following questions, giving people 1–2 minutes to answer each question:

- What roles do I play in positive youth development?
- How do I hope to have an impact on young people?
- How do I hope to have an impact on my colleagues?
- Why am I a part of this group?

Ask participants to share components of their starpeople with their table group.

Wrap-up: Note the many different hopes, dreams, and goals that people have shared. What are some of the common hopes, dreams, and goals?

Key Elements: Communication, Working Together, Team Building, Celebration, Vision

Asset Categories: Support, Boundaries and Expectations, Positive Values, Positive Identity

Insider's Tip: For a group that works together regularly, you can use this as an introductory activity that leads into naming group goals and focus.

YOUTH CONTINUUM DIALOGUE

Purpose: To help participants explore and share in a nonthreatening way their beliefs, perspectives, and values about youth work

Estimated Time: 20 minutes

Supplies: None

Directions: Describe the process of a continuum dialogue to the group: You will read two opposite statements, and participants will place themselves somewhere on an imaginary arc between the two statements. Designate one end of the arc for the first statement and the other end for the second statement. Read aloud one set of statements, and allow everyone to choose where to stand on the arc.

Once everyone has made a choice of where to stand, ask for volunteers to explain why they chose their positions. As with any group activity, participants should show respect, give full attention to the people who are talking, and not challenge or tease them. And, as people listen to and reflect on what's been said, they can change their minds and move to different positions. If they want to say why they moved, give them an opportunity to do so. Encourage participants to be honest and to consider what they are most likely to do on a daily basis rather than what they *think* they should do. After they have finished explaining their positions, read aloud another set of statements and again allow participants to find their places on the arc. Repeat as often as you wish.

Choose from the following options the continuum dialogue statements that best reflect issues your group needs to explore.

(a) Youth at this age learn best through a variety of activities offered based on their multiple intelligences.	(b) Youth at this age learn best by digging in deep on one focused activity.
(a) Youth at this age learn best from experiential learning.	(b) Youth at this age learn best from instructive/didactic/theoretical learning.

(a) Youth at this age learn best in unstructured, imaginative play.

(b) Youth at this age learn best in highly structured, directed play.

(a) Youth thrive when they are grouped with people of similar styles and backgrounds.

(b) Youth thrive when they are grouped with highly diverse groups of peers.

(a) Youth at this age learn best when they are given time and space for reflection and processing of what's happened.

(b) Youth at this age learn best when they are on the move.

(a) The development of the character and morality of young people is the responsibility of the family.

(b) The development of the character and morality of young people is the responsibility of the community.

(a) I think our youth have plenty of opportunities to give voice to what happens in the program.

(b) I don't think our youth have adequate opportunities to be resources in the program.

(a) I do my best work with smaller groups of youth.

(b) I do my best work with masses of youth around me.

(a) It is better to deal with disciplinary issues as they arise.

(b) It is better to clearly articulate rules and consequences upfront.

(a) Outcome-based programming clearly captures what is going on in our program.

(b) Outcome-based programming misses some of the human dynamics of what is going on in our programming.

Wrap-up: This is a great process for digging deeply into issues and really learning from each other.
- What new insights did you gain? What gave you food for thought from this activity?
- What potential application do you see from what we've talked about?
- How might your new understanding have an impact on your work?

Key Elements: Communication, Conflict Resolution, Creative Problem Solving

Asset Categories: Support, Positive Values, Commitment to Learning, Empowerment, Boundaries and Expectations

Insider's Tip: This activity can be used to see where staff teams stand on issues and to provide a safe dialogue space for them to hear each other out on issues that concern the group. It should not be used as a method for voting on an issue, but it can be used to encourage dialogue and to solicit input and opinions.

Inspired by the continuum dialogue developed by Marylyn Wentworth and expanded and enriched by many facilitators in the National School Reform Faculty, www.nsrfharmony.org. Used by permission.

FIVE CRITICAL ELEMENTS

Purpose: To solicit input, wisdom, and best practices from all participants regarding a given issue

Estimated Time: 30–60 minutes

Supplies: Paper, pens, possibly copies of research papers (depending on the topic), sticky notes (the big size), marker for each table group

Directions: Ask participants to work individually to list their top five critical underlying principles when it comes to working with youth: "Given your expertise, experience, and research, what are the five nonnegotiable things that you believe youth should experience/need/gain when they are involved in your program/agency?" Give them 5 minutes to record the nonnegotiables when it comes to their work—the "must haves" or all bets are off.

When time is up, ask participants to share their lists in groups of four to seven people. What are the critical ingredients that need to be part of our work? Ask someone at each table to jot down any common elements, principles, or themes mentioned in their group. After everyone has shared, ask the table groups to narrow down a list of their top five critical elements as a group, including as many contributions from each participant as possible. Remind them that the goal is to find the five elements we can commit to as a team to provide our youth no matter where they are in our program/agency/community (pick the correct setting based on who is in the room). Give them 10 minutes to discuss.

When time has expired, ask each table group to write each of its five top elements on a sticky note and post the notes on a wall for everyone to see. (They should use the markers and write in large print.)

Look over all the sticky notes as a big group and link similar elements. Try to clump them into five "buckets" by clustering the sticky notes on different areas of the wall. Name each cluster, keeping in mind that the group is trying to determine five critical elements for the whole agency (or vision or program).
If there is time, develop the five critical elements into statements: these are the five things to commit to as a team/community to provide *all* youth served.

Wrap-up:
- What did we accomplish together?
- How do you feel about the work we did?
- What are you excited about as you look at the ideas we generated?
- How do we keep these ideas alive and keep this work moving forward?
- What do we need to do to ensure that these critical elements are available for all youth?

Key Elements: Communication, Working Together, Vision, Conflict Resolution, Creative Problem Solving

Asset Categories: All

Activity contributed by Laura Hansen, Nashville, Tennessee

BUILDING BRIDGES

Purpose: To help participants think about the importance of communication and input in casting a vision

Estimated Time: 40 minutes

Supplies: Interlocking building blocks (such as Legos), space to spread out, blueprint (drawing of bridge)

Preparation: Use the blocks to construct a bridge that teams can build. Make a diagram of the bridge to create a "blueprint." Prepare a separate but identical set of blocks and a copy of the blueprint for each team.

Directions: Break the big group into three teams. Each team is composed of *engineers*, *builders*, and *messengers*. For instance, if you have 18 people in your group, you will have three teams of 6 people, and each team will have two engineers, two builders, and two messengers. The goal is for the three teams to accomplish the building project within the specified amount of time, without breaching the parameters given. The teams will be competing against each other to complete the project first.

For each team, the engineers get the blueprint; they will be in a different room or at the far end of the room with their backs to the builders. A team's builders sit at a table with the blocks. The messengers are the communication and information conduit between the builders and the engineers. Only the engineers can see the blueprint, and only the builders can touch the blocks; neither engineers nor builders may leave their area. The messengers are free to move about, and may carry information in both directions, but they may not touch the blocks or see the blueprints.

Send each of the groups to their designated spaces. Then, take engineers from all three teams into a room to give them their instructions for the game. Then give instructions to the messengers from all three teams. Then give instructions to the builders from all three teams. Allow 20 minutes for the teams to build the project, then compare blueprints and projects to measure their success.

Wrap-up: Was this task difficult? Ask each job-specific group the following questions:
- What was the hardest part about doing your job?
- Did you devise a strategy to overcome your difficulties? What was it?

Ask the big group these questions:
- Were you successful? Why or why not?
- What could have brought the team more success?

Completing the task isn't the definition of success. If you only got halfway done but had clear communication and your group was working well together, then you were successful and on your way to completing your project.

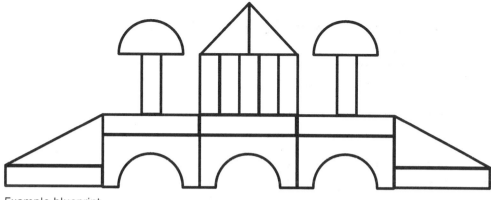

Example blueprint

- How do you see that the building project is similar to casting a vision, communicating in your team, and getting things done in real life?
- In this game, the engineers had the vision but the builders had the tools. How is this an analogy for community work?
- Which role do you most identify with in your current position and work? Can you see some of these same obstacles in your current job?
- What are some tricks to communicating effectively and reaching the vision you set?

Key Elements: Vision, Communication, Working Together, Teamwork, Creative Problem Solving

Asset Categories: Support, Empowerment, Social Competencies, Boundaries and Expectations

Insider's Tip: This task is a communication challenge that is hidden in an enjoyable building project.

Activity contributed by Bill Van de Griek, Nashville, Tennessee

DECLARATIONS OF PURPOSE

Purpose: To give participants an opportunity to articulate and commit to a vision of hope for building strong relationships

Estimated Time: 15 minutes

Supplies: A writing utensil and paper for each participant

Directions: Ask participants to take a few minutes to think about the *best* relationships they've had or have with young people. What qualities made up those relationships? What made them good? What made them special or enjoyable? Ask them to jot down a few notes.

Next, invite participants to think about what they can draw from those relationships to apply to other youth that they work with. Invite them to pair with a partner to discuss the following questions. How can they move the needle on those other relationships to make them better? How can they be more intentional in building them up? What can they learn from what they did in the good relationships that they might replicate in others?

Finally, ask participants to identify one or two things from their great relationships that they want to commit to action in other relationships. Ask them to complete one or two of the following promise statement starters:

I am . . .
I do . . .
I believe . . .
I focus . . .
I engage . . .
I help . . .
I regularly . . .
I pay attention to . . .
I make . . .
I try . . .
I work . . .
I say . . .
I point out . . .
I celebrate . . .
I will . . .

Wrap-up: Ask participants to share what they've written with the people at their table and to talk about the strong relationship they are trying to replicate. This will serve as a public declaration of their intentions.

Key Elements: Vision, Communication, Celebration

Asset Categories: Positive Values, Positive Identity, Empowerment, Social Competencies

CAN OF WORMS

Purpose: To allow people an opportunity to get on the same page and explore their expectations

Estimated Time: 10–15 minutes

Supplies: A jar or can

Preparation: Write questions and the corresponding options for responses (see "Sample Questions for Youth Workers" below) on slips of paper, and put these questions into the jar or can.

Directions: We all draw the line in the sand in a different place with expectations, and this activity will let us explore what we consider normal expectations and see how they compare or contrast with others. Have six or seven volunteers line up. Ask one of the volunteers to pull a question from the can and hand it to you. Read the question out loud, along with the three or four responses that accompany it. Then reread the responses slowly, inviting each volunteer to step forward when you call out the answer that reflects his viewpoint.

Sample Questions for Youth Workers:
- What is the most effective environment for encouraging a child to learn/study?
  (Worksheets? Skills-based computer games? Group-learning activities? Field trips? Service-learning?)
- Where should we invest the majority of our daily programming time?
  (Academics? Character building? Team building? Play? Leadership development? Personal development? Career exploration? Serving others?)
- How do you want young people in our program to treat you?
  (Boss? Friend? Parent? Teacher? Coach?)
- What is a healthy amount of screen time (computer, video games, television, phone) for youth each day?
  (0–2 hours? 4–5 hours? 8+ hours?)
- What is a healthy amount of physical activity for youth each day?
  (30 minutes? 1 hour? 2 hours? 4 hours?)
- How can youth workers most powerfully affect youth behavior?
  (Discipline? Consequences? Redirect? Incentives?)
- How available should I be for my work?
  (Traditional paid work hours? All day: 8 a.m.–10 p.m.? 24/7? Other: _____?)

Sample questions for a PTO or parent group:
- What is a reasonable bedtime for a 10-year-old on a school night?
  (7 p.m.? 8 p.m.? 8:30 p.m.?)
- What is an appropriate age for a child to have a cell phone?
  (8? 10? 12? 14? 16?)
- What is an appropriate age for boys to go on a first date?
  (12? 14? 16?)

- What about girls?
  (12? 14? 16?)
- What is an appropriate curfew for girls on a school night?
  (8 p.m.? 10 p.m.? Midnight?)
- For boys on a school night?
  (8 p.m.? 10 p.m.? Midnight?)

If appropriate, talk about differences in gender expectations for various life issues.

Youth Samples: Using questions like these with children and teens can help you find out the norms for their lives at home and also help them discover their boundaries within your group.

- How much time do you spend playing video games after school?
  (0–2 hours? 4–6 hours? 8 hours?)
- How much time do you spend doing homework after school?
  (30 minutes or less? 1–2 hours? 4–6 hours? 8 hours?)
- How much time are you involved in active play (running around, getting your heart pumping)?
  (30 minutes or less? 1–2 hours? 4–6 hours? 8 hours?)

Wrap-up: The can of worms may show that we have different norms in our work, our homes, or our programs. Everyone agrees that we need certain boundaries, but not everyone agrees where those boundaries should be. This activity is just a conversation starter for talking about boundaries for our group. We can't assume that we all see things the same way. We have to talk about boundaries to see where we all stand and where we're all coming from.

Variation: With this variation, you get to choose the can of worms that you want to discuss. Break into smaller groups, each of which pulls one question out of the can of worms to discuss as a group. Invite them to talk about the questions and discuss ways to handle the issues. Have each group share its issue and ideas with the big group. Use this to role-play sticky situations: *Here's the situation. What would your response be?*

A sample way of choosing what worms are put into the can is to make all the issues about personal safety—dealing with bullies, dealing with strangers, dealing with real-life potential dangers:

- You smell smoke in the house. What's the first thing you do?
- A stranger shows you a picture of a dog and asks you to help find the dog. What do you do?

Make sure the issues are appropriate for the group.

Key Elements: Creative Problem Solving, Conflict Resolution, Communication, Community Building

Asset Categories: Boundaries and Expectations, Support, Empowerment, Social Competencies, Commitment to Learning

Activity contributed by Cindy Lawrence, Nashville, Tennessee

PICTURE PERSPECTIVES

Purpose: To gain perspective on participants' vision for youth work

Estimated Time: 10–15 minutes

Supplies: Postcards or random pictures (abstract, nature, objects, people) downloaded from office.microsoft.com/en-us/images/ (these are free-use images) and printed on 5" × 7" paper, or purchase a deck of card images from the Center for Creative Leadership (www.ccl.org)

Variation: Instead of postcards or images, use a variety of objects (a lightbulb, a puzzle piece, a can opener, rosary beads, a knitting needle, etc.).

Directions: Ask participants to look at all the images and pick one. Which one speaks to them about their work with youth right now (or about their leadership, issues in their work, etc.)?

Ask participants to get into groups of three or four and talk about why they selected their images. What do the images say to them about their work?

Invite participants to select a second image, looking this time for one that speaks to them about *what could be* with their work (or leadership, issues, etc.). Which one says something to them about their vision and hopes? Ask participants to find their same group of three or four people and talk about the images they selected.

Variation: Using the first set of instructions for selecting an image, ask people to think about their project or their work and invite them to write a headline that goes with the picture they selected and describes where they are.

Wrap-up: Sometimes we need a new perspective—to look at something in a new way. Focusing on young people's strengths and trying to replicate them requires a different perspective, one that calls for an intentional effort to look for gifts and strengths, highlighting them and building on them.
  - When you looked at your image, what did you see?
  - How do we move from our current activities to our vision of where we could be?
  - How do we make our ideal the real?

Key Elements: Communication, Vision, Celebration, Community Building, Team Building

Asset Categories: Constructive Use of Time, Support, Positive Identity, Social Competencies, Positive Values

Adapted from an activity contributed by Janice Virtue, Durham, North Carolina

VISUAL THINKING

Purpose: To help individuals and groups think about group vision; to discover new ideas or help people identify their goals

Estimated Time: 15 minutes

Supplies: Two colorful pictures or posters large enough for everyone to see easily; paper and a writing utensil for each person

Directions: Distribute paper to all of the participants and ask them to divide their papers into quarters by drawing a vertical line and a horizontal line.

Show the first picture to the group, and ask them to quickly think of two or three descriptive words that come to mind when they see the picture. If the picture is a mountain scene, participants might choose descriptors such as *lavish*, *breathtaking*, or *peaceful* (but not just *mountain*). Ask them to write those words in the top left quadrants of their papers.

Show the second picture to the group, and ask them to think of two or three words that come to mind when they see the picture. Each person should write those words in their bottom left quadrants.

Explain that this activity is going to let thoughts sneak in through the back of their minds, like those great thoughts that come when you're sitting in traffic or singing in the shower.

Tell the group that the question to explore is "How can we empower youth to lead more in our organization?" An alternate question might be "How do we need to strengthen the way we work with young people?" Use whatever question the group needs to discuss. This activity works particularly well for brainstorming solutions to challenges.

Participants use the words they wrote in the left-hand columns along with the group's question to trigger thoughts that they record in the right-hand columns. For example, if one of the words on the left side was *colorful*, one hope for empowering youth to lead in the agency might be "to really listen to the colorful ideas and personalities of our young people in figuring out ways they want to be more involved in our agency." Ask the group to share another example, and then give everyone a few minutes to complete the exercise.

Wrap-up:
- What were some of the thoughts that surfaced during this exercise?
- What hopes do you have?
- What goals, personal agendas, and aspirations did you see?
- What will you remember about this activity?

Key Elements: Communication, Vision, Working Together, Team Building, Creative Problem Solving

Asset Categories: Empowerment, Boundaries and Expectations, Commitment to Learning, Constructive Use of Time

REDESIGNING YOUR COMMUNITY

Purpose: To identify specific strategies to help communities be more conducive to youth development and seek the best interests of youth every day

Estimated Time: 15–20 minutes

Supplies: Ten sheets from a self-adhesive flip chart (such as 3M Post-it chart paper), colored markers

Preparation: Label each flip chart sheet with one of the following sample titles or personalize the activity by creating sheets that speak specifically to your audience (for example, for teachers you might target school areas such as "in the classroom," "on the school bus," and "in the hallways"). Place the sheets and markers around the room.

Sample Titles: "In schools," "In congregations," "Among businesses," "For parents/families," "For adults/mentors," "For law enforcement officials," "For any organization," "For government agencies," "For child-care providers," "For the media," "In neighborhoods."

Directions: Ask participants to think of specific ways to make their communities more intentional about helping to nurture young people and then pretend that they have the power to redesign their communities. Each flip chart sheet represents one of the 10 areas they may redesign.

Give participants the following instructions:

a. Look at all the areas and choose the three that most interest you.

b. Take a few minutes to think about what specifically you would like to do in these areas to make them more youth-friendly and youth-inviting. Think creatively; don't be limited by traditional ways of doing things. What can you do physically, emotionally, and socially to promote and nurture youth in this part of your community? Ponder as you walk around the room looking at the charts.

After a few minutes, ask participants to move to one of the areas they want to redesign. When several people have gathered by a sheet, choose one person to record ideas, and ask everyone to share thoughts with the recorder.

Give participants about 5 minutes per station or area to discuss and record. Call "time" to signal when the 5 minutes are up and it is time for them to move to another station. This activity can create a lot of conversation, so be careful to watch the time.

Reconvene the larger group and choose several volunteers to share ideas from each of the community areas.

Wrap-up: Each part of our community can become a place to encourage healthy youth development. It just takes our creativity, willingness, and dedication to spread these very important messages to people like teachers, business owners, neighborhood organizations, media representatives, and law enforcement officials.

- What ideas did you hear that resonate as something that is needed, doable, and/or valuable?
- What message do you want to communicate with someone after doing this activity? With whom will you share it?

Key Elements: Vision, Communication, Community Building

Asset Categories: Constructive Use of Time, Support, Empowerment, Positive Values, Positive Identity, Commitment to Learning, Boundaries and Expectations

MASTER BLUEPRINTS

Purpose: To provide participants with a creative outlet to express their feelings, pride, and concerns about their work

Estimated Time: 10–15 minutes

Supplies: Paper, crayons or markers

Directions: Invite participants to draw something that represents their program (or agency). They can use symbols, draw a picture, or sketch a floor plan—whatever suits them best. Within their pictures, they should include both strengths and challenges. Ask them to personalize their pictures in some way by denoting what they think makes their program (or agency) special and what they value most about it.

Give participants 5 minutes to draw, and then ask them to form groups of four to share their pictures and talk about what they drew.

Variations: Instruct participants to form pairs and then draw the young person who enters their building/program and the young person who leaves their building/program.

Draw the culture of the school/program/agency; a picture of the town you want to live in; the ideal high school/community, plus the current school/community (do this last option as part of a visionary or comparison process).

Wrap-up: Some of us hem and haw about being asked to draw, yet there is no value judgment, no good or bad. We're scared we won't be good at it, scared we're not good enough. Say, "I didn't ask you to create art. I merely asked you to picture something, to draw something."

Why is picturing important? Mention the following if no one says it: Picturing helps us envision what we're working toward in a way that words can't capture. It helps us visualize the "it" we want to make happen. Visualization often adds depths and dimensions to a process that words alone won't capture.

- What encouraged you as you listened to each other share the things that are special to you about your programs/agencies?
- The work we do has challenges. We know them well. It is important to uphold the things we value to help us maintain balance and perspective. What helps you maintain hope and value in your work with youth?

- How do you help young people know and see their own worth, value, and what makes them special—despite their own challenges?

Key Elements: Communication, Vision, Celebration, Community Building

Asset Categories: Constructive Use of Time, Positive Identity, Support, Positive Values, Social Competencies

Insider's Tip: We know how to use words and may even know the right words to say. Getting people to think in pictures can open up a whole different part of the brain. In groups, drawing pictures usually gets a good laugh, it sometimes humbles everyone (particularly when individuals have to present artwork and explain it—people can be timid of drawing), and it helps people think in new ways about what is possible.

Includes input from Anderson Williams, Nashville, Tennessee

JANITOR STORY

Purpose: To illustrate the power of the group to have an impact on the larger community

Estimated Time: 5 minutes

Supplies: None

Directions: Tell the group, "We're going to work together to give some people a gift today, so I need you to follow my instructions. Sit up straight in your chair. Scoot all the way to the front of your chair. Scoot all the way to the right of your chair. Scoot to the back of your chair. Scoot to the left of your chair. Now do one more big circle—to the front, right, back, left. Great job! Do you know what we just did? We just cleaned every one of these chairs for the cleaning crew!"

Wrap-up:
- How long would it have taken one person to clean the surfaces of these chairs?
- How long did it take us to clean the chairs?
- What happens when we pool our time, talents, and resources toward a common goal?

Let's pledge to use our collective power to make great things happen around us!

Key Elements: Communication, Working Together

Asset Categories: Support, Empowerment, Boundaries and Expectations, Social Competencies

Activity contributed by Travis Wright, Washington, D.C.

RAINSTORM

Purpose: To close a meeting with a reminder that the group has the power to work miracles when we all work together toward a common goal

Estimated Time: 8–10 minutes

Supplies: None

Directions: Demonstrate a series of motions while the group is completely silent and simply watches and listens. Go through the following motions, spending a few seconds on each before moving on to the next: rub your hands together back and forth, tap one index finger on the palm of your other hand, snap the fingers of both your hands, then drumroll (tap) both your hands on your thighs.

Stop and ask the group if they could tell what sound you were trying to make through all the motions. If they say "rain," then affirm their answer. If they don't guess rain, tell them to keep thinking.

Round one: Now lead them through the same series of motions you just demonstrated. All players stand in a circle. When you make eye contact with a player, he starts doing the same action that you are doing—rubbing his hands together, for example—and continues until you signal a change in action by making eye contact and modeling a new action. Go around the circle making eye contact with each player, silently signaling each of them to mimic the first action. When you get all the way around the circle, signal the players one by one to change to the finger tapping on the palm. This process continues as you take the players through each motion—rubbing of hands, tapping fingers, snapping fingers, drumroll—and then reverse the order, from drumroll to snapping fingers to tapping fingers to rubbing hands to quiet. After going through all the motions, ask the group again, "What sound did we make together?" See if they guess rain. If they don't, then prompt them to think about nature and the sounds they just made.

Round two: Ask the group, "What could we do to make this sound more like a thunderstorm?" If they say, "Add thunder," ask how they could simulate thunder. If they suggest adding lightning, ask how they could simulate lightning. Then try to make a rainstorm together with the new additions to the "orchestra." Don't forget that you'll need to be the one to cue the thunder and the lightning. (For thunder, you might designate four or five players to jump up and down or stomp their feet. For lightning, you might have someone flicker the lights, flash a flashlight, or flicker window shades—whatever will create a sense of light vs. dark.)

Wrap-up: We achieved a miracle together—we made rain! With just one person, the sound isn't anything special. You can't tell that you made rain. But when everyone worked together, how did it sound? With everyone working together, we made a miracle. What else can our group accomplish if we work together?

Key Elements: Working Together, Vision, Community Building

Asset Categories: Support, Boundaries and Expectations, Empowerment, Social Competencies, Positive Identity

Adapted from Great Group Games for Kids *by Susan Ragsdale and Ann Saylor with contributions by Cindy Lawrence, Nashville, Tennessee*

WAVES OF CHANGE

Purpose: To help participants realize the impact they can have by using their gifts and talents to help others

Estimated Time: 10 minutes

Supplies: One piece of card stock and a writing utensil for each person; a 9" × 13" dish or roasting pan containing one inch of water (if your group is large, form teams of 15–20 and give each team a pan of water); tape

Directions: Give all participants a piece of card stock and ask them to write the answer to the following question: "What difference do you want to make, and what is the gift you want to pass on to people you work with?"

When they're done, ask them to roll up their cards to resemble long straws and secure them with tape.

Ask participants to gather around the dish or pan of water and, on your count, blow gently through their straws to make waves in the water.

Wrap-up: These waves are symbolic of the waves of changes that happen when you share your gifts with the people around you. The more intentionally you use your gifts (blow through the straws), the bigger the effect (waves) you will have on your community (the pan of water). Blowing individually, you have a small effect on the water, but working together you can make huge waves—huge effects. Remember to work together toward your common vision of using your gifts and talents to support the people around you.

Let participants take their straws home as a reminder of the impact they can make on others.

Key Elements: Vision, Celebration, Working Together, Team Building, Community Building

Asset Categories: Support, Empowerment, Social Competencies, Positive Identity, Positive Values

PEARLS

Purpose: To help participants realize the importance of sharing wisdom with the group and gathering wisdom from the group

Estimated Time: 10 minutes

Supplies: One pearl bead for each person, one bowl (option: choose colored beads or marbles for a varied selection)

Directions: At the end of your meeting, invite each participant to think of one pearl of wisdom to encourage the group as they move forward in their work. Ask everyone to gather in a circle around the bowl, and give each person a pearl. Invite participants to share their pearls of wisdom, and then put their pearls into the bowl.

Wrap-up: After everyone has spoken, tell the group that the bowl symbolizes the collective wisdom and strength of the group, all of us working together toward a common goal.

Invite everyone to pick a pearl out of the bowl to take away as a reminder of the strength of the group.

Key Elements: Community Building, Vision, Celebration

Asset Categories: Support, Empowerment, Positive Identity, Positive Values

Adapted from an activity by Marilyn Peplau, New Richmond, Wisconsin

TOAST FOR CHANGE

Purpose: To close a meeting with a commitment to action

Estimated Time: 5–10 minutes (depending on group size)

Supplies: A small cup for each participant, including yourself; something good to drink like sparkling cider or juice

Preparation: Fill cups with sparkling cider or juice.

Directions: Tell participants that you would like everyone to join in a toast. Distribute the filled cups and ask the group to form a large circle. Offer a toast similar to this: "I hope that all the people in this room will take a look at themselves and use their unique strengths to support our group."

Invite others to make their own personal toasts about positive changes they hope the group will make to support one another and the youth you work with. After each toast, the group says "Cheers," lifts their glasses to the person who offered the toast, and takes a sip of juice.

Wrap-up: Teacher Erin Gruwell made a toast for change with her students in California. You might know Gruwell and her students from their having been depicted in the movie *Freedom Writers*. A toast for change was an invitation to a second chance, a new start.

Invite participants to give second chances and new starts freely as they work toward the vision and hopes they hold for the young people around them.

Key Elements: Celebration, Vision, Communication, Community Building

Asset Categories: Support, Empowerment, Positive Identity, Social Competencies

RADAR COMMITMENTS

Purpose: To close a meeting with a commitment to action

Estimated Time: 5–10 minutes

Supplies: Three Post-it Notes per person

Directions: Tell participants to think about what they want on their radar screen when they go home. What do they want to do with what they learned from your time together? Ask each person to write down a commitment to action on three Post-it Notes (the same action on each note).

When everyone has finished writing, tell the group that two of the Post-it Notes are for them to post at home and at work for several weeks to serve as visual reminders to keep their action commitment on their radar screens.

Ask participants to jot down some form of contact information, e-mail or otherwise, on the third Post-it Note, and then invite them to find partners, talk about their commitments, and exchange Post-it Notes. In two weeks, they will check in with each other to see how they're doing on their commitments.

Wrap-up: Things come and go on our radar. To make the changes we wish to see, to have the impact we want, requires us to pay attention and deliberately put on our radar screens thoughts that we don't want to lose.

Ask for a few people to share what's on their radar from this time together.

Key Elements: Celebration, Vision, Communication, Community Building

Asset Categories: Support, Empowerment, Positive Identity, Social Competencies

Activity contributed by Marilyn Peplau, New Richmond, Wisconsin

ASSET PLAN(E)S

Purpose: To help participants form a network to support their commitments to making a difference in young people's lives

Estimated Time: 10 minutes

Supplies: Sheets of brightly colored paper in six or seven different colors, writing utensils

Directions: Distribute colored paper to participants and invite them to think about their own roles in the lives of youth (or think about what they want to apply from the meeting or training). Instruct them to record on the paper their name, organization, some form of contact information (preferably e-mail or snail mail), and their commitment to action.

When everyone is done, instruct the group to make airplanes out of their sheets of paper, helping each other as necessary.

Gather the group into a circle, everyone facing the middle, and have participants throw their paper airplanes into the middle of the circle. Ask everyone to find an airplane that is a different color than the one he or she made and take it along without telling whoever made it who has it. In a month, participants send notes of encouragement to the people whose airplanes they took.

Wrap-up: Do you know what allows a plane to glide in the air? The wings. The wings manipulate air pressure to lift the plane and keep it balanced. Sometimes, we need a "lift" or a "boost" from someone who knows what it's like to do the very important work that we do. As we leave, we make a commitment to hold our airplane person's work and commitment in our thoughts over the next month, and then contact him in some way to say that we support him and are cheering him on.

Key Elements: Vision, Celebration, Working Together

Asset Categories: Support, Social Competencies, Positive Identity, Empowerment

Insider's Tip: This activity works best with groups of 15 or more and builds in accountability within the group.

COLORFUL COMMITMENT

Purpose: To close a meeting with a commitment to action

Estimated Time: 5–10 minutes

Supplies: Various colored 3" × 5" note cards, writing utensils

Directions: Give participants one card each and ask them to record their commitment to action on their cards. Instruct them to hold their cards next to their "control center" (head, elbow, knee, heart, etc.)—whatever they perceive to control their actions. Then they hold the action cards in the air, crumple them or fold them up while they're in the air, then put the cards in their purses or pockets and take them along.

They keep their cards nearby until they carry out their commitments. Then they can recycle the cards (literally, or by passing on the idea of the action to someone else in a "pay it forward" spirit).

Invite participants to share their commitment with one other person in the room.

Variation: Distribute index cards in four different colors to organize participants into groups of four—either all one color, or one of each color—to talk about their commitments.

Key Elements: Vision, Celebration, Working Together, Communication

Asset Categories: Support, Social Competencies, Positive Identity, Empowerment

Activity contributed by Jim Conway, Madison, Wisconsin

GEOMETRIC REFLECTION

Purpose: To close a meeting with a reflection on what participants learned

Estimated Time: 5–10 minutes

Supplies: Chart paper

Preparation: Draw the following shapes down the left side of the chart paper: a cartoon speech bubble, a circle, a square, and a cloud. On the right side of the paper, write four incomplete sentences that correspond with the shapes:
(Cartoon speech bubble): *Something that is bubbling up within me . . .*
(Circle): *Something that keeps going around in my head . . .*

(Square): *These two things square with my belief . . .*
(Cloud): *I've been wondering about . . .*

Directions: As a closing reflection, ask participants to pick one of the images with its connecting statement and complete the sentence out loud. If there are more than twelve people in your group, divide them into groups of four for this activity.

Key Elements: Vision, Celebration, Working Together, Communication

Asset Categories: Support, Social Competencies, Positive Identity, Empowerment

Activity contributed by Marilyn Peplau, New Richmond, Wisconsin, and Jim Conway, Madison, Wisconsin

COINS

Purpose: To reflect on what participants have learned from their time together

Estimated Time: 5–10 minutes

Supplies: A penny, a nickel, a dime, and a quarter

Directions: Hold up the coins. Note that they represent the four lowest monetary units in the United States and Canada: a penny, a nickel, a dime, and a quarter. Ask the group what the total value is.

Say, "The number of assets needed for youth to thrive is 40. Together, these coins equal 41 cents. They add up together to make up 40 and 1. One makes the difference. In our work with youth and each other, one person makes the difference. What we do matters.

"The smallest change is no small change. Look at the words on the back of the U.S. penny. The Latin phrase, *E pluribus unum*, means 'Out of many, one.' Among the many people who make a difference, I might be that one. Forty assets plus one person equals a world of change."

Wrap-up:
- What was your nickel's worth in this training? (One small thing you're taking home from the training.)
- What was your dime's worth? (A medium thing.)
- What was your quarter's worth? (A critical thing you want to remember.)

If you wish, give participants 41 cents each; tell them it is your investment in them and challenge them to share with others.

Key Elements: Vision, Celebration, Working Together

Asset Categories: Support, Social Competencies, Positive Identity, Empowerment

Activity contributed by Marilyn Peplau, New Richmond, Wisconsin

MOVING THOUGHTS

Purpose: To close a meeting actively, with an energetic commitment to action

Estimated Time: 5–10 minutes

Supplies: None

Directions: Invite participants to find partners and stand face to face—this is called the "front to front" position. Next have partners stand with their backs to each other—the "back to back" position. Then ask the partners to stand next to each other, facing in the same direction—the "side to side" position.

Have partners practice assuming the different positions. Call out each one to make sure they have all three moves down.

Tell them that you're going to play a game and that partners must stand in whatever position you call out. Start slowly with the three different moves. Two more commands to know: "share" and "switch." When you call the "share" command, give the partners a question to discuss. When you call the "switch" command, everyone must find a *new* partner within 5 seconds; do a 5-second countdown and make a big deal about it—be loud and build it up to keep energy flowing.

Start slowly and randomly call out the various moves: front to front, back to back, side to side. Gradually speed up the tempo and keep calling out variations. Switch several times to provide opportunities for people to mingle. When participants are front to front, let them share for 90 seconds—do this two or three times before switching partners.

Sample sharing format:

First time: name and agency/school/program

Second time: name, agency/school/program, and the best thing about working with youth is . . .

Third time: name, agency/school/program, and one thing you're walking away from this meeting/training with is . . .

Key Elements: Vision, Celebration, Working Together, Communication

Asset Categories: Support, Social Competencies, Positive Identity, Empowerment

Insider's Tip: This activity can be used as an icebreaker that is simply active and fun with no processing—just sharing—or as an icebreaker focused on the subject of discussion. Or it can be done as a closing at the end as a way for participants to share their commitment: what are they walking out with?

Activity contributed by Jim Conway, Madison, Wisconsin

INDEX

ACTIVITY	PAGE	SUPPORT	EMPOWERMENT	BOUNDARIES AND EXPECTATIONS	CONSTRUCTIVE USE OF TIME	COMMITMENT TO LEARNING	POSITIVE VALUES	SOCIAL COMPETENCIES	POSITIVE IDENTITY
30-Second Spotlight	27	●	●		●	●	●		●
Animal Corners	76	●		●				●	●
Asset Clusters	44	●	●	●	●	●	●		●
Asset Matchups	51	●	●	●	●	●	●		●
Asset Plan(e)s	119	●	●				●		●
Behind Every Name	19						●		●
Big World, Little World	26	●	●			●	●		●
Box In, Box Out	98	●	●	●					●
Boxes of Risk	95	●	●	●			●		●
Building Bridges	104	●	●	●			●		
Can of Worms	107	●	●			●	●		
Cars	90	●		●		●	●		●
Coins	121	●	●				●		●
Color Focus	16			●			●		
Colorful Commitment	120	●	●				●		●
Community Puzzle	84	●		●		●	●		
Connections	18	●					●		●
Corner Choices	28			●			●		●
Curious Questions	21	●					●		●
Declarations of Purpose	106		●			●	●		●
Diversity Bingo	29	●	●		●		●		●
Diversity Buttons	83	●	●			●	●		●
Each One Teach One	74	●	●		●	●	●		●
Electric Current	93	●	●	●			●		
Exploring Perspectives and Viewpoints	36	●	●	●		●	●	●	
Five Critical Elements	103	●	●	●	●	●	●	●	
Four-Letter Words	65	●					●		●
From Troubles to Treasures	88	●	●		●	●		●	
Geometric Reflection	120	●	●					●	●
The Great Escape	72			●	●		●		
Gum Ball Count	77	●	●	●					●
Intersections	61	●						●	●
Janitor Story	114	●	●	●			●		
Listening Concentric Circles	30	●		●		●	●		
Master Blueprints	112	●			●	●	●		●
Missed Signals	40	●		●		●	●		
Mission to Mars	75	●	●	●	●	●	●		

ACTIVITY	PAGE	SUPPORT	EMPOWERMENT	BOUNDARIES AND EXPECTATIONS	CONSTRUCTIVE USE OF TIME	COMMITMENT TO LEARNING	POSITIVE VALUES	SOCIAL COMPETENCIES	POSITIVE IDENTITY
Mixed Messages	85		•				•	•	
Moving Thoughts	122	•	•					•	•
Mumble Jumble	94	•		•	•		•		•
My Starperson	99	•		•			•		•
Name Tag Sandwich	17	•	•	•				•	•
Never Judge a Book by Its Cover	82	•						•	•
Obstacle Walk	91	•	•	•				•	
Paper Amy	64	•		•				•	
Pearls	117	•	•				•		•
People, Places, Things	43	•			•	•	•		
Picture Perspectives	109	•			•		•	•	•
The Potluck Name Game	20	•						•	
The Power in My Hands	41	•		•			•	•	
Professional Lineups	54	•		•	•		•		•
Quick Thinking	48	•	•	•	•	•	•	•	•
Radar Commitments	118	•	•					•	•
Rainstorm	114	•	•	•				•	
Redesigning Your Community	111	•	•	•	•	•	•		•
Road Signs	69	•		•			•	•	•
Scribble Sketches	46	•	•	•	•	•	•		•
Sentence Puzzles	38	•	•	•		•			
Shields in Battle	49	•	•	•					•
Shifting Gears	86	•	•	•		•	•		•
Social Shuffle	71	•		•			•	•	
Sparks Speedy Conversations	62	•	•		•				•
Strong Suits	33	•	•	•			•	•	•
Tabletop Conversation Starters	22	•						•	•
Tandem Thinking	47	•	•	•	•	•	•	•	•
Team Continuum Dialogue	59	•	•	•		•	•		
This is a WHAT?	78	•	•	•			•	•	
Tiny Teach	73		•		•	•		•	
Toast for Change	118	•	•					•	•
Tower Assets	42	•	•	•	•	•	•	•	•
Train of Clues	23		•					•	•
Transformation Stations	89	•	•				•	•	
Trick or Treat with the Assets	45	•	•	•	•	•	•	•	•
True Headings	31	•	•	•				•	•

124

ABOUT THE AUTHORS

Susan Ragsdale and **Ann Saylor** are two of Search Institute's best-selling authors. As nationally recognized trainers and consultants in the youth and community development field (including career highlights with the YMCA of the USA, Point of Light Institute, 4-H, Harpeth Hall School, HandsOn Network and Volunteer Tennessee), they coach youth-serving agencies and schools on developing and empowering youth leaders, team building, service-learning, program strategies, and youth development best practices through the Center for Asset Development at the YMCA of Middle Tennessee. They draw upon 36+ combined years of positive youth development experience to create inspiring, effective resources and workshops for parents, teachers, and youth workers.

In addition to providing professional development to the field, Susan and Ann follow their passion for books and are noted authors. Besides *Get Things Going*, they have published, four other books that maximize experiential learning and play with purpose:

- *Building Character from the Start: 201 Activities to Foster Creativity, Literacy, and Play in K–3* (Search Institute Press)

- *Great Group Games: 175 Boredom-Busting, Zero-Prep Team Builders for All Ages* (Search Institute Press)

- *Great Group Games for Kids: 150 Meaningful Activities for Any Setting* (Search Institute Press)

- *Ready to Go Service Projects: 140 Ways for Youth Groups to Lend a Hand* (Abingdon Press)

Susan and Ann began to use games and play as a platform for learning early on in their lives. They have fond memories of teachers who made learning fun by playing games such as "Spelling Baseball" and "History Jeopardy." Realizing that most people learn more effectively when they're active, experimenting with new behaviors, and solving challenges, they started integrating experiential learning techniques in classrooms, camps, and conferences. As a 14-year-old summer sports camp counselor, Susan created wacky games to keep the campers—only two years younger!—moving and having a good time. Ann started her games collection when she was 17. Neither dreamed that folders filled with games would one day lead to opportunities to write books.

Visit Susan and Ann's website and blog at www.TheAssetEdge.net, and send your favorite games, tips, and ideas to them at cad@TheAssetEdge.net. You can stay connected through Twitter @TheAssetEdge, Facebook at The Asset Edge, or LinkedIn via Ragsdale or Saylor.